Intelligence

in the Workplace

CATHERINE McGEACHY

First published 2001 by
Veritas Publications
7/8 Lower Abbey Street
Dublin 1
Ireland

Email publications@veritas.ie
Website www.veritas.ie

ISBN 1 85390 529 1

Cover design by Pierce Design
Printed in the Republic of Ireland by Betaprint Ltd, Dublin

Veritas books are printed on paper made from the wood pulp of
managed forests. For every tree felled, at least one tree is planted,
thereby renewing natural resources.

To my Mum,
whose love, support and prayers
have made the content of this book possible.

CONTENTS

FOREWORD

I have written the book in such a way that it can be read in short snippets – on the plane or during a busy schedule – to facilitate my colleagues in industry who are beleaguered by mounds of paperwork, books and reports to read and who have asked me to 'keep it simple and short'.

I have also aimed to make it immediately practical with a 'How to' section, personal stories, comments on what specific companies are successfully doing in this area and dangers to watch out for. I share my own thoughts on the two issues I see facing the business world, in the Afterword.

ACKNOWLEDGMENTS

I would like to thank my assistant, Colette O'Grady, for all her hard work in organising my research and for the many extra hours she worked to ensure that this book met its printing deadlines. I would also like to thank all those whose prayers strengthened me as I worked on the book and for the insightful comments and support of Editor, Toner Quinn.

CHAPTER I

WHY IS THERE AN INTEREST IN SPIRITUALITY AT WORK?

A mind once stretched by
a new idea, never regains
its original dimensions
– Oliver Wendell Holmes

There are many reasons for the exponential interest shown today in the topic of spirituality and spirituality in the workplace. I have found several themes emerging time and again: *corporate downsizing; the impact of current business philosophy on environmental degradation and social disintegration; corporate cultures based on the economic value system; the fact that there is less time for spiritual and community connection external to work; waning influences of Church, civic groups and the extended family; the fact that the kind of people a company has and what the company stands for are becoming just as important as what it sells; the special interest taken in the subject by people in powerful decision-making jobs; baby-boomers (those born in the 1940s) are seeking meaning in life; the discovery that external rewards can diminish internal motivation; the realisation that organisations don't transform themselves – people do; the need for open, honest communication; the realisation that creativity and innovation are critical to the success of the millennium company; the bottom-line benefits of looking after employees; employee opinion; public opinion; the number of books, articles and seminars on the subject; increase in interest in Eastern Philosophies; advances in science and healthcare; the emergence of spiritually-related data from scientists; the increased awareness among the public of the environment and of natural disasters; pressures of modern society leading us into the 'sixth extinction'; the different type of age that we are living in; the need for a new corporate evolutionary imperative.*

Let's have a look at these reasons in some detail.

(1) Corporate downsizing

Corinne McLaughlin is a co-founder and Executive Director of the Centre for Visionary Leadership in San Francisco. She is a lecturer, author and adviser to former President Clinton's Council on Sustainable Development. In her work and research[1], she has noted that corporate downsizing and greater demands on remaining workers have left them too tired and stressed to be creative. This, she says, is happening at a time when globalisation of markets requires more creativity from employees and research is showing that organisations must offer a greater sense of meaning and purpose for their workforce if they are to retain them.

Corporate downsizing began in the US in the early 1980s and in the 1990s in rock-solid companies such as IBM. The current collapse of demand in the telecommunications sector in the US has fuelled another run of downsizing since 2000 in related industries and their suppliers, not just in the US but around the world. The resultant uncertainty and vulnerability have caused employees in the US in the 80s/90s and now employees all over the western world not just to fear losing their jobs but to question the value of their work and to seek comfort in spirituality.

Reem Creations[2] documents that managers believe that spirituality in corporations is rapidly emerging because of the overall feeling that the American workplace has become an insecure and uncomfortable environment to work in. 'The downsizing, reengineering and layoffs of the past several years have transformed corporate America into a pretty unfriendly place....' Technology is becoming more difficult to comprehend, support staff is declining and everyone is expected to perform at optimum levels. Of course, the American workplace is all over the world because American multinationals have sites all over the world. So, 'the pretty unfriendly place' has crept into many countries. In fact, one HR Director told me that their company and another company formerly celebrated for its innovative HR practices and wonderful work environment have become 'positively reptilian' as a result of downsizing, drastic cost-cutting measures and a values-shift firmly focused on 'bottom line'. The National Speakers' Bureau, in an article entitled 'Spirituality in the Workplace',[3] documents that many organisations, faced with severe funding challenges, have squeezed as much as they can out of cost cutting and finding more efficiencies, leaving their people drained and in acute need of spiritual repair in their workplace. Writer and consultant Peter Grazier[4] calls today's workplace 'toxic', describing it as more hectic than ever and commenting that 'downsizing and rapid technological changes have left their marks in precious little time for family, friends and outside activities. As a result, as employees stretch themselves thin trying to perform, the ability to balance one's life is moving higher on the charts as a characteristic desired in the workplace.'

(2) The impact of current business philosophy on environmental degradation and social disintegration

Former trial lawyer Joseph Jaworski, who is currently Founder and Chairman of the Centre for Generative Leadership, writes about the 'anti-leadership vaccine' that college students received in the fifties and sixties. 'I don't recall one college professor or one mentor ever talking to me about leadership or about giving something back or about serving others.'[5] In Ireland, there has been a strong culture of serving and giving back to society. In terms of giving financial aid, Ireland spends more per capita than the US and many other European and Western countries[6]: this is a country founded on 'as long as you do it to the least of these, you do it to God'. However, Ireland is succumbing to the influences of the consumer culture and as Professsor Danah Zohar of Oxford University and psychiatrist and psychotherapist Ian Marshall have discovered, 'Western-type culture, wherever it is found on the globe, is awash with the immediate, the material, the selfish manipulation of things, experience and others... Our spiritually dumb culture is a victim culture.'[7]

These authors lament the fact that western society downgrades human qualities in favour of hyperactivity and that 'We dreadfully neglect the sublime and the sacred within ourselves, others and our world... In a spiritually dumb culture, our motives become distorted: the social and economic pressures that surround us urge us to mistake wants for needs and they urge us to want more than we need, to want constantly and insatiably.' Such a culture sees success not in emotional terms and certainly not in spiritual terms. Instead, success in the consumer culture consists of power, more of everything that appeals to the senses and an immediate gratification. Immediate gratification pulls the individual away from their spiritual core, from that part of them that can provide meaning, true nurture, lasting beauty and joy. Consequently, the person becomes fragmented within and unhappy, and because s/he is disconnected with reality this person usually sees the cause of their problems as 'out there' instead of 'in here' – inside of them. So, this person engages in blame. This is one of the reasons why our western culture is a 'victim culture'.

Our high-tech industry has spawned many successes over the years and has made many employees wealthy. However, even young, talented employees are not entirely happy with their lot. Professor Ian Mitroff of University of Southern California who is also President of consulting firm Comprehensive Crisis Management, and Elizabeth Denton, a New York based organisational consultant, describe meeting employees in a successful Silicon Valley software company. These employees were not quite thirty years of age yet were millionaires, had interesting and fulfilling jobs – up to a point. When asked about their jobs and lives, they ' were vaguely disconsolate, despairing – something "beyond words" one told me: "something missing".'[8]

Our consumer culture has trained us to be dependent on material 'scaffolding' for our sense of value, meaning and confidence: factors such as house, car, position in the organisation, number of people we are in charge of, wealth, possessions, physical shape, looks, education, colour, and mixing with celebrities, have all become surrogates for genuine self-esteem, confidence and meaning. We even have in our vernacular the phrase 'bad hair day' – reflecting that someone is having an off day! Such 'scaffolding' isn't bad in itself. It only becomes problematic when we begin to depend on it for our value and meaning. What if some of the props disappear as in when there is a crash on the Stock Market and billions of dollars are wiped off stocks. What is our reaction to losing our money? Or when we age, our skin is not as fresh or our body is not as beautiful (we think). What is our response to this? Or we have worked hard to achieve a Masters degree only to discover that it is not considered 'currency': that we need yet another Masters or even a PhD. How do we respond to this? And how do we respond when we have been trained to obtain our self-esteem and meaning through our job and so give twelve plus hours to the job each day only to discover that a downturn in the economy somewhere else means I lose my job? Usually, we become painfully aware that this scaffolding we have been using to buttress our fragile self-esteem and lack of meaning has masked deep-seated fear which we should have been facing. Had we faced our fears on an incremental basis, we would have been strong enough to cope when a prop was removed. However, having succumbed to the prop, we experience the gripping fear and anxiety that has lurked there within us all along. We also experience the aching emptiness, the lack of fulfilment and meaning that the prop has been hiding from us. In some cases, when faced with losing a prop, we cling more intensely to it. 'Some of the props are psychologically and even physically addictive' notes Peter Vaill, one of the top ten organisation development specialists in the United States, 'and when our reliance on a prop for meaning reaches this stage, we are moving beyond chronic fear and anxiety into an actual life-threatening condition.'[9]

In the past twenty years, Ireland has succumbed to the value system I have described above. How has it happened that a country with a living experience of *'meitheal'* – a community helping one another out – has abandoned that value in its corporate world? The answer, I believe, is primarily in the performance management systems used in that corporate world and in the vulnerable willingness of the Celt to unquestioningly accept the contents of those systems. For example, Church and State ruled Ireland's everyday life – its moments and seconds – up until twenty years ago. Church and State are two strong hierarchies and we know that in hierarchical structures, people beat to the drum of their boss. Whatever 'tune' that boss wants the person to play, they will play it. So, when performance management systems – based as they were not on cooperation, community and team (the Irish culture) but on competition, isolation and individualism – were introduced into the American multinationals sited here in Ireland, they were unquestioningly embraced. These systems asked peers, subordinates, suppliers and superiors to rate an employee, and on that rating the employee was awarded a bonus and extra shares. Only so many in a team would get the bonus and the number (if any) of share options allocated depended on what one's rating would be. So what happened? Many employees told me that there was 'no way' they would favourably rate a colleague in case that colleague would 'do them out of' their bonus and share options. Thus began the sad break up of some of the best qualities of Irish culture as the Celt was trained to value money, competition, individualism and selfishness. It is fascinating to note that the very qualities that were thrown out – cooperation, community and team ('we' instead of 'I') are now heralded by those monitoring successful companies (see the section on 'Bottom Line') as crucial to survival in these demanding economic times.

Richard Barrett was formerly the Values Coordinator at the World Bank and founder of the World Bank Spiritual Unfoldment Society in 1993. He is now an international consultant supporting leaders throughout the world in building cultural capital and strengthening human resource capacity. His research and experience have shown that 'The issue of trust, or more precisely the lack of trust, lies at the very heart of the difficulty that organisations have in mining the creative potential of their employees. Ill-managed re-engineering and downsizing created cultures of fear. By focusing uniquely on corporate fitness, i.e. productivity and efficiency to improve corporate survival, organisations have ignored their most important requirement for success – the trust of employees.'[10] As M.U. Hart summarises, 'Such psychological co-option is necessary because of high job insecurity and because deteriorating social relations at the workplace have created a psychological vacuum. What is called for is a psychological, mental and behavioural preparation for living with instability and for being able to think of oneself in terms of renewable, exchangeable.'[11]

Peter Grazier[12] describes the general workplace as 'toxic' and describes some of the elements of a 'toxic work environment':

1) Contracts in some US companies require people to give the company the right to fire an employee any time for any reason. Obviously, the new employee will not feel a strong loyalty or motivation to a company with this value system.

2) Many companies have short-term contracted staff, who are essentially self-employed, rather than burdening themselves with the extra costs of full-time employees. The free-agent employee can often feel isolated and at the mercy of organisational 'fickleness'.

3) Employees in companies that have downsized often find they are doing the work of their colleagues who have now gone. Flexitime in such an organisation can mean working any 15 hours you want. The problem with increased working time, Grazier notes, is that it forces the employee to choose between two competing obligations – work life and personal life (or family) – creating inevitable guilt in either direction.

4) Rewards given to the privileged: 'pay and bonus systems for those at the top have escalated to Hollywood star status, frequently in the absence of corporate performance', says Grazier. Obviously, such an inequity tears out loyalty and motivation from employees.

5) The issue of labour as an expense instead of an asset. Many organisations insist that their employees are their most important asset and then go on to measure that asset so that they can determine how much it is contributing to the bottom line on a per hour basis. However, in the light of this, executives are surely working with a value systems that sees employees not as an asset to be developed but as a cost to be minimised.

6) Closely associated with this last point is the business of viewing of employees as an up-datable resource rather than in terms of a human being with unique experiences, hopes, wishes and dreams.

7) The ubiquity of technological devices such as the mobile

phone, notebook computers, pagers and email, have had a significant impact on the quality of an individual's life. In the past, when such technologies did not exist, people had more quiet time, time to think and to be. Now, work enters the home and social environment, often uninvited. Can a person really give his/her full attention to those s/he is with if s/he is expected to be so easily contactable and if work can be so easily transported into the home or a social setting?

One of the most challenging commentaries on the impact of current business philosophy on environmental degradation and social disintegration comes from the Japanese Science Council, set up by Prime Minister Junichiro Kiozumi.[13] The Council comprises eminent professors from the various universities in Japan whose remit was to identify why Japanese policies on the Environment and Education were not working. The Council's research led to the conclusion that it is not just the Japanese who should be concerned, but all nations: '…the problems are ones which affect the human race in its entirety and which should, therefore, be addressed at the global level.' The Council found that by 2050 there will be no human race or living planet left if we continue being driven by our consumerist lifestyle that requires a huge energy consumption to fuel it and if populations continue to increase at their current levels. 'The 20th Century has seen human civilisation essentially reach the pinnacle of its pursuit of wealth and material comfort (with social systems) predicated on an orientation towards materialism and energy… It is these social systems which have resulted in destruction of the natural environment and now threaten to undermine the future well-being of the human race. The human race must choose between two alternatives: do we maintain present modes of production and life styles predicated on an orientation towards materialism and energy and sacrifice much of our world in the process or do we strive to ensure the future of humanity by developing new modes of production and life-styles that involve a shift away from the materialism-energy orientation?' The report says the fact that we are losing our ability to recognise what it is to be human (our 'human dignity and self-worth') only exacerbates the gravity of the problems it outlines.

(3) Corporate cultures based on economic value systems

In his book *Playing for Keeps*, author and organisation design consultant Frederick Harmon, founder of Synthesis Consulting, sums up the limitations of and damage created by the focus on bottom line: 'Remember our Four Commandments: Make Money, Grow Fast, Watch the Numbers, Stay out of Corporate Trouble... They will not appear in the budget or in the manager's performance appraisals, yet together, they form an invisible sieve, draining profit dollar by dollar.'[14] Why does this value system prevail? The reason lies in our assumption, from an economics point of view, of what drives the human being. Says writer Francis Fukuyama[15] 'The entire imposing edifice of contemporary neoclassical economic theory rests on a relatively simple model of human nature... that human beings seek to acquire the largest possible amount of the things they think are useful to themselves, they do this in a rational way and they make these calculations as individuals seeking to maximise the benefit of themselves before they seek the benefit of any of the larger groups of which they are part. In short, neoclassical economics postulates that human beings are essentially rational but selfish individuals who seek to maximise their material well-being' Fukuyama notes that the great economist Adam Smith believed that people are driven by a selfish desire to better their condition but he did not believe that economic activity could be reduced to purely selfish and mercenary motives. Fukuyama refers to this when he talks of neoclassical economics being 80% correct in its view that the human being is self-interested, but that it cannot account for the other 20% of human behaviour. That other 20%, he says, is deeply embedded in social life and it cannot be understood apart from the customs, morals and habits of the society in which it occurs. He points out that people have been known to run into burning houses to save others, die in battle, or throw away lucrative careers so that they can commune with nature somewhere in the mountains and if wars were fought simply over economic resources, then there would not be nearly as many of them.

However, wars normally involve non-utilitarian goals like recognition, religion (values), justice, prestige and honour. Liberal democracy works, Fukuyama says, because the struggle for recognition, justice, prestige, honour and religion (values) is now pursued on an economic battlefield, not the military battlefield of former eras. Where once princes risked their lives in battle in order to conquer their enemies, they now risk their capital in order to build industrial empires.

If we apply this understanding of the rationale for battle to modern business, we realise why financial benefits are not the sole motivator for employees – even though they may seem to be on first glance. We can also see that by working to meet the needs in people for recognition, values, justice, prestige and honour, we may well have less organisational politics and so enhance productivity, efficiency and creativity. If these needs are met, then the employee's eyes are on the business ball rather than on fighting his/her own values battleground. Consequently, full employee attention and energy can be focused on making the business work. However, in our society, economists – according to Fukuyama – form the main voice lauding the benefits of the pursuit of narrow self-interest through the market because they believe that the greatest good to society as a whole can be achieved in this way. And this voice has, by and large, prevailed.

Business princes have risked their capital in what Peter Vaill calls the 'get control, sell off, get out' type of buyout in which

133,219

the princes are 'not concerned about whom they hurt as they prey on the organisation's resources. Their view is exploitative; they are raiders. They treat the organisation as a financial object, as a "cash cow" … an instrument for those who are strong enough to get control of it.' Vaill calls this model of the organisation the material-instrumental (M-I) model because the company is valued only for its financial worth and people are valuable only in so far as they contribute to that financial worth. 'In this model, people are viewed as part of the physical assets of the company, being "material human resources" or a "talent pool" – they are viewed as static, timeless and unchanging' which Vaill calls a psychological absurdity because 'people are infinitely varied and constantly changing'. The organisation, he says, is instrumental because its *raison d'être* is solely to achieve the objectives of its owners.[16]

While the asset battle is on, those the princes leave in charge of their camps rigorously pursue the lauded value of self-interest. Writer and consultant James Autry puts the modern battle for prestige in this way: 'Who knows how long business will be suffering the destructive residue of a generation of gunslinger superstar CEOs who, in their excessively narrow definition of "stockholder value" have created workplaces of fear and anxiety? The only salvation of the workplace as a source of personal meaning and purpose is to develop and reinforce manager-leaders who will embrace the values of Robert Greenleaf (i.e. Servant Leadership).'[17]

The impact of a purely economic value system on building highly committed human resource management practices is clearly pointed out by Professor Jeffrey Pfeffer of the Stanford Graduate School of Business. He notes that 47% of companies researched had difficulty getting top management's attention; that 56% of companies said that their corporate culture did not emphasise human resource issues; and 69% experienced a lack of support from middle management. Professor Pfeffer also points out that 61% of companies researched experienced lower morale among the remaining work force after downsizing.[18]

International marketing and trade expert Ann Coombs[19] takes a look at the notion of 'success' in the twenty-first century and challenges the wisdom of the purely economic value system in a company. Will profit continue to matter above all else, she asks? Is it a company's responsibility to nourish spirituality? Can there be a human wholeness in business, she wonders? Alan Pritz, founder and president of Inner Resource Enhancement talks of the 'slash and burn' economics of the 1970s–1980s and 2000/2001 and how they have generated prolonged stress.[20] Prolonged stress is dangerous because, according to stress management pioneer Dr Hans Selye, this consumes one's finite supply of 'adaptive energy' and once this is gone, you die.[21] As long as we still have some adaptive energy supply after prolonged stress, we will experience consequences of the stress that are less extreme than death but still extremely serious. So, the employee who has experienced prolonged stress experiences burnout, consequent absenteeism, medical leave and the organisation faces high turnover costs. In this context, Ann Coombs asks whether the business based on economic value is really reaping the profits it could.

Cheryl Belles[22] points out that 'Business and leadership training often focuses on strategy and results with a heavy financial orientation, creating managers who view such efforts as re-engineering and process improvement as merely scientific, mechanistic processes. We, as employees and consumers, ask our organisations to think about the long-term yet we demand short-term returns on our investments. We, as consumers and investors, drive companies to reject proposals that promise long-term benefits in favour of monthly or quarterly financial returns. Consultants often, therefore, focus on selling events versus generating small catalytic reactions aimed at a larger change process.'

When we consider that work consumes not just 8-10 hours per day but includes preparation and travelling time, then that figure easily becomes 11-13 hours per day if not more. Those who own their businesses will work far more than an eight-hour day and young qualified doctors in their first year in hospital work on average 16 hours per day and then have preparation and travelling time on top of that. So, work consumes close on 50% of our active life. On this basis alone, it is in everyone's interest that a more balanced system than the economic value system be used.

Family and community life are built around values that support the good of the whole. When people go to their place of work, they search for this same set of values. In the US, where there is a highly mobile society, 'community' is not necessarily as strong as in the very 'rooted' society of Ireland. Yet, research (see section on 'Employee Opinion') shows that even people in a very mobile society look for a workplace that shares their value system. The mismatch of personal and corporate values is perhaps, according to Richard Barrett,[23] the most pervasive problem facing companies today. Obviously, if most organisations are functioning on the basis of economic value alone, then the employees will be faced with either subscribing to a value system of narrow self interest and all the negative politics and the consequent lack of trust that go with that value system *or* going against the tide, standing up for their values and perhaps having to leave the company altogether. This latter choice requires facing fear which requires courage. Facing fear is, in itself, a stressful process, but it is less stressful than the former choice which consigns the employee to a work environment in which there is little participation, negligible empowerment and no one feels safe (how can they if there is no trust?).

When there is no alignment between personal values and organisation values, an inner schism takes place: our logic is driving us in one direction while our inner being, our divine centre, is prompting us to go in another. The conflict we face is whether to satisfy the needs of the ego (security, relationship, self-esteem) or the needs of our divine centre (truth, integrity and trust). If we allow this schism to continue over a protracted period of time then our behaviour will begin to reflect conflict in a host of ways: irritability, confusion, blame, frustration and anger.

When the things we value are not valued by those with whom we work, we may engage with our colleagues, but we will withhold what we are truly thinking and feeling. In other words, we will not be operating honestly with them. Ultimately, to protect our sense of self, who we are, we will detach, and once we detach our heart is not in the job. We have lost our motivation. We are working at half-mast. The company is paying for full productivity but we can only give it fifty per cent. We lose and the company loses.

The focus on economic value alone has triggered a haemorrhaging of western companies to cheaper sites in Asia, for example, thus destabilising the economies left behind. In Ireland, the arrival of peoples from other countries offering inexpensive labour has caused several small companies to discontinue the contracts they had with their existing labour force in favour of the newcomers. Trends like these cause insecurity, anxiety and fear.

In the US, the separation of Church and State is enshrined in Amendment 1 of the Constitution. In Ireland there has been a closer link between the two groups. Values – spiritual values – would still be evident in the Irish workplace. As Limerick businessman, Dan O'Connell, used to say 'You never take maximum profit – you always leave some for the other man.'

(4) Less time for spiritual and community connection external to work

Given the very long working day that many people are experiencing, it is understandable that their involvement in church/mosques/temples/extended family/community groups has come under pressure. Today's employee is trying to fit many essential and meaningful tasks into a diminishing window of time and, in doing so, has found that some tasks have become casualties. The result? People have become disconnected from their traditional spiritual, family and social communities and are forced to see their workplace as the source of the nurture they received from these communities. So, they bring their faith practices and belief systems to work and look to work to provide the feelings of relatedness, belonging and feeling 'cared for'. So, the workplace is being experienced as a source of spiritual strength and connection to others.

(5) Waning influences of church, civic groups and extended family

Closely connected to the workplace as the source of spiritual strength is the fact that formal religion no longer holds sway, and the concept of 'family' has changed due to the fact of divorce and remarriage with some children missing one parent and others, whose mothers/fathers have entered several relationships, having siblings from those several relationships. Danah Zohar and Ian Marshall put it this way: 'We are under stress today about questions of right and wrong, about how to keep ourselves on a straight path and how to guide our children. Formal religion and its ethics no longer hold sway, family structures are fluid and constantly changing and our sense of community and tradition has broken down. Somebody has moved all the moral goalposts and we don't know any longer what game we are playing, never mind what constitutes its rules.'[24] For some people, the workplace is providing them with the only consistent link to other people and the basic human needs for connection and contribution.

(6) What kind of people you have and what your company stands for are becoming just as important as what you sell

Fukuyama comments that 'One of the most important lessons we can learn from an examination of economic life is that a nation's well-being, as well as its ability to compete, is conditioned by a single, pervasive cultural characteristic: the level of trust inherent in the society.'[25] Corinne McLaughlin notes that the best talent seeks out organisations that reflect their inner values and provide opportunities for personal development and community service, not just bigger salaries.[26] 'In the next century,' she says, 'a company will stand or fall on its values as the best talent are drawn to companies with good values...'.[27] Lewis Richmond[28] (former Buddhist monk turned catalogue software tycoon, and author of *Work as a Spiritual Practice*) points out that Buddha himself found enlightenment out of a 'serious case of job dissatisfaction' as an Indian prince some 2,500 years ago. The CEO of Rockport Shoes openly talks of spirit and encourages employees to spend work time imagining how they can reflect in practical terms their deepest selves in their work. The Cone/Roper Trends Report of 1999[29] documents that three out of four consumers polled say they're likely to switch brands associated with a good cause if price and quality are equal, and in another poll,[30] 79% of graduating MBA students across 50 graduate business programmes said that a company should consider its impact on society in such areas as the environment, equal opportunity, family relationships and community involvement. According to Professor Verschoor of the University of Chicago, spirituality and profitability are not mutually exclusive: companies with a defined corporate commitment to ethical principles do better than companies that don't make ethics a key management component.[31]

(7) Spiritual interest from people in powerful decision-making jobs

Spirituality has been studied by many groups in nations all over the world for thousands of years. According to Judith Neal, Director of the Centre for Spirit at Work at the University of New Haven in Connecticut, one reason for the growing acceptance of the notion of spirituality at work is that 'more and more CEOs and high-level managers are coming out of the closet about their own spirituality.'[32] For example, Monsanto CEO Robert Shapiro, who meditates twice a day, was not at all embarrassed when word leaked that he had led a three-day meditation retreat for 15 of his top executives – an event that has evolved into five similar programmes at the St Louis-based multinational. Senior executives are in a position to influence corporate culture change and this top-down organisational influence, coupled with the current popular interest (see sections on 'Employee and Public Opinion') is creating a healthy foundation and conduit for spiritual pursuits to root and grow.[33]

(8) Baby boomers seeking meaning

Consultant and former inspirational sports coach Abe McLaughlin believes that interest in spirituality at work will continue because 'many Americans – especially baby boomers (those born in the 1940s) – have attained a measure of affluence through their work and are now seeking more meaning in their lives, including at the place where they spend most of their waking hours.'[34] 'They've gotten all the toys and now there's that yearning to satisfy themselves spiritually,' says Janice Gamache, a Washington-based consultant with the Institute for Reflective Leadership. International speaker and consultant on spirituality in the workplace, Martin Rutte notes that the baby boomer generation has entered its 50s and has been looking at those issues that are characteristic for this age – issues such as: the legacy and long-term values that they want to leave behind; the areas of life they would like to focus on now that they have reached the peak in their career; new priorities as they watch older generations of their family die. Rutte comments that while these kinds of thoughts are usual for people in mid-life, what is unusual is that the baby boomer generation is so large: 'When it begins to think about these issues, then society follows. As spirituality emerges for baby boomers, the whole of society is affected.'[35]

(9) The discovery that external rewards can diminish internal motivation

Alfie Kohn writes and speaks widely on human behaviour, education and social theory. In his article 'Challenging Behaviourist Dogma: Myths About Money and Motivation'[36] he notes studies which found that employees who were given an incentive for doing a task actually did lower quality work than those given no reward at all. 'Workers' internal motivations are actually diminished by the introduction of such external rewards. Also, when the workforce is more focused on what has to be done to get a reward than the importance of the work itself, there is no ethical connection to the quality of the work produced and no spiritual satisfaction to be derived from it, further reducing intrinsic motivation.'

(10) The realisation that organisations don't transform themselves – people do

Professor Robert Quinn of the University of Michigan Business School makes the statement that 'We can all manage the world, but we must first change ourselves.'[37] Individually, he says, we can contribute to the transformation process. Joseph Jaworski highlights the difficulty of anyone being able to effect change in another or in a system because we look at others and life through our filters: 'Most of what we "see" is shaped by our impressions, our history, our baggage, our preconceptions. We can't see people as they really are because we're too busy reacting to our own internal experiences of what they evoke in us.'[38] So, we rarely actually relate to reality: instead, external factors evoke in us software from our personality, culture, traditions and experiences. Just as neoclassical economics sees the human being as a fixed item – a finite resource – so, too, Jaworski says, we are controlled by an 'ironclad grip' which 'maintains the illusion of fixity... I don't see you – I see the stored-up images, interpretations, feelings, doubts, distrusts, likes and dislikes that you evoke in me.' So, the challenge is for us to learn to see reality more as it is, that is to clear out the filters of our own histories, our own needs and the interpretations that our personalities, culture and traditions give us on reality. Then, instead of reacting to reality from deep-seated filters, we would be choosing how best to respond in the situation. Cleared of cultural, historical and experiential identities, our sense of who we truly are would change. We would begin to relate to others in a more authentic way and, in so doing, facilitate them in responding from a more authentic place in themselves. To clear these filters out requires going deep inside ourselves and that is a spiritual journey.

Such a journey will be challenging because we are re-scripting our values: we are looking at what interpretations our personality, culture, traditions and experiences have given us and then we are choosing whether or not to accept those interpretations. We become the meaning makers for our lives and rediscover the ability to turn a job into a vocation, the ability to see magnificence in the everyday, the ability to look at something/someone familiar with fresh eyes, the ability to make the most out of every situation. This is true empowerment: the freedom to choose how we will respond in a situation/to a person. So, change management isn't something that is applied to me from outside of me. It is about how I interact with people and circumstances, becoming aware, in those moments of interaction, of old software that is being evoked in order to be removed. It is about realising that the circumstances I am in and the people I am with are the best change management tools I can have because these will be the factors that trigger in me awareness of garbage software and these will be the factors that provide the opportunity for me to change that software. Organisations do not transform themselves – it is the people within an organisation who transform themselves. As Irish novelist James Joyce wrote in his biographical novel, 'Welcome, O life! I go to encounter for the millionth time the reality of experience and to forge in the smithy of my soul the uncreated conscience of my race.'[39] In a dramatic admission, Ian Mitroff and Elizabeth Denton admit: '...we have been forced to a painful conclusion: by themselves, all of the conventional (change management) techniques in the world will not produce fundamental and long-lasting changes. At best, conventional techniques produce only partial changes, which erode over time so that most organisations revert to their initial problem states or they work for only a tiny fraction of organisations.'[40]

(11) The need for open, honest communication

As individuals focus on their inner spiritual journey of clearing their filters and changing themselves from within, they become more real, more authentic. This sparks a need for open, honest communications in the workplace. Martin Rutte says 'When the truth is allowed to be safely and respectfully spoken, old problems clear up, new possibilities emerge and people feel more aligned. They work together in a trusting team.'[41] Without their filters, people can create a 'safe space' in which others feel permission to talk about their truth without fear of judgement and reprisal. So, in business, there are those who are already on their spiritual journey, clearing their filters, changing within and, therefore, looking for this open, honest communication. There are others who haven't even begun this journey. Consequently, there is a pressure from within the business system to start people on that journey so that real change and true communication can take place in order that the untapped performance potential of employees and owners can be released.

(12) Creativity and innovation – critical to the success of the millennium company

Albert Einstein said 'The problems that exist in the world today cannot be solved by the level of thinking that created them.' This is a challenge to business and society to think differently. However, the only way that people will allow themselves to think differently is if there is an atmosphere of trust. We have already seen from Francis Fukuyama that wars have been started over issues of recognition and honour. Thinking differently can expose an individual to ridicule. So, organisations must create a safe environment and this means an environment of trust. But according to Richard Barrett, trust can only come about when everything a company does is rooted in values that are practised as a habit, not on a whim. He has also found that in order to tap the truly deep layers of creative potential in people, the work those people do must be seen by them as meaningful.[42]

Some organisations have thought that by taking their people through a mission, vision, values process, the full creative potential in employees would be released. They have found this not to be the case because most contemporary education – and certainly the consumer culture – schools people in the art of survival, promotion and success strategies, each of which pulls the individual away from their deeply creative centre. So, organisations must address this issue by creating a working environment supportive of creativity and innovation. This means introducing employees to that part of them in which the deep reservoirs of creativity reside: their spirit. It also means making this spirit dimension of the employee a normal feature of the workplace.

The global marketplace has become very competitive. In Europe, prices are denominated in the Euro as opposed to the national currency of the trader. So, greater transparency of price now exists in the 'Euro-zone'. The Internet has made comparisons of prices across economic zones very simple. In such a competitive marketplace organisations have to give their products a competitive edge by enhancing existing services or designing entirely new products. This requires a creative workforce. Spiritual exercise puts people in touch with the source of their creativity. It allows them to generate an intuitive feeling about products, services and the organisation.

(13) Bottom-line benefits of looking after employees

'What is the source of all profit?' Fred Harmon asks. 'Certainly not the numbers. The numbers are only symbolic representations of corporate performance. In any company, the real source of profit is the thousands of individual actions by individual employees. Add value to each of those acts and you add profit. The aim of corporate values is to add that value, in every act, all the time.'[43] Francis Fukuyama writes that for liberal political and economic institutions to flourish, they must have a healthy and dynamic civil society that cooperates effectively across all diversities.[44] Ian Mitroff and Elizabeth Denton found in their audit of corporate America that a key determinant of a successful bottom line is spirituality. They found that employees connected to their spiritual centre outperformed their 'disconnected' colleagues and concluded that spirituality may well be the ultimate competitive advantage. However, most employees in this audit did not know how to connect to their spiritual centre or how to effectively apply that part of their equipment to their workplace.[45]

In *The 100 Best Companies to Work for in America*,[46] writers Robert Levering (co-founder of the Great Place to Work Institute, Inc.) and Milton Moskowitz (journalist and chronicler of socially responsible business) describe how companies are recognising that it is good business to share ownership and profits, to care for the physical and emotional needs of employees and their families, to provide opportunities for personal growth and advancement and to support the local community and serve humanity. A survey by the Economist Intelligence Unit[47] ranked human performance ahead of productivity and technology as a source of competitive strength. In the same survey, the ability to attract and retain the best people is seen as the primary force influencing business strategy by 2005. In a case study of Sears Roebuck,[48] *Harvard Business Review* documents that for every 5 unit increase in employee attitude, a company can drive in excess of a twofold increase in customer impression which drives a 1.5 times increase in revenue growth. The study shows that if an organisation makes itself a compelling place in which to work, it becomes a compelling place for customers and ultimately turns the organisation into a compelling place in which to invest. *Business Week*[49] notes that 39% of US investors say they always or frequently check on business practices, values and ethics before investing. Global consulting firm William Mercer undertook a 'Work/Life and Diversity Initiatives Benchmarking' survey.[50] This survey shows that a growing number of organisations are focusing on the common good: 86% of the organisations said they could not compete in the 90s work arena without addressing work/life and diversity issues. More than half of the survey respondents believe work/life programmes positively affect employee morale, attendance, productivity, recruitment and bottom line. A study undertaken by Michael Cox and Michel Rock[51] found that for jobs of low, medium and high complexity, highly motivated employees were respectively 52%, 85% and 127% more productive than employees who had average motivation. When the comparison was made between the most motivated and the least motivated employees, the level of productivity was 300% more for low complexity jobs, 1200% more for medium complexity jobs and so large that it was un-measureable for high complexity jobs. A Gallup Poll[52] of 55,000 in the US found that four attitudes when taken together, correlate strongly with higher profits. These attitudes are: workers feel they are given the opportunity to do what they do best every day; workers believe their opinions count; workers believe their fellow workers are committed to quality; and workers have made a direct connection between their work and the organisation's mission. In a similar vein, David Cole[53] comments that as a Director of the company Software Plus, he was astonished to discover that almost all of his staff shared the same spiritual belief system and that this deep common ground really helped them in their relationships with one another. Having a unified world-view and a larger connection in order to achieve their potential as a group had been powerful motivators for his people. Another survey[54] shows that as workers feel a sense of satisfaction and a belief that their work is meaningful, the motivational influence of salary and benefits becomes less important. In a study of 'Business Performance, Employee Satisfaction and Leadership', involving 14 organisations and 25,000 employees in the US, the Wilson Learning Corporation[55] found that approximately 39% of variability in corporate performance was attributed to the personal satisfaction of the employees based on a range of indicators. The same study found that 69% of the variability in personal satisfaction was attributable to the quality of the employees' relationship with their manager and their manager's empowerment skills. So, identifying and managing employees' emotional needs is a key competence for the contemporary leader looking to enhance the bottom line.

Wayne Jackson[56] speaks of studies which have shown that employees who work for organisations that encourage spiritual values are less fearful, less likely to compromise their values and have more focus and motivation on the job. Corinne McLaughlin[57] cites the fact that public shaming of Nike's sweatshop conditions and slave wages paid to overseas workers led to a 27% drop in its earnings in 1999, and details another study by the pioneers and global leader in staffing services, Robert Half International. This study concluded that CEOs should spend about 34% of their time building the morale and productivity of their staffs – a process described by Robert Haas, CEO of Levi Strauss, as 'doing well by doing good'. So, it is clear that if staff are happy, they will be more productive, more creative and will enjoy a greater sense of fulfilment. Personal fulfilment and high morale are closely linked to outstanding performance and, therefore, have a direct impact on an organisation's financial success.

(14) Employee opinion

So what factors are affecting employee happiness? The answer to this question is clear from the following comments: 'There have been massive layoffs; I'm asked to do more with less; I don't see an end to the tunnel with this; the job market isn't great, so I'm stuck here; there is a malaise and a tiredness and corporate officers know that';[58] 'I'm tired of having constantly to park my soul at the door before I go into my organisation'; 'Organisations are constantly wanting and demanding more and more of us all of the time. But they can't have it both ways. They can't have more of us without getting and nourishing the whole person. Organisations must give back and contribute as much to the whole person as they want in return.' 'Organisations feel free to beat up on us forty to sixty hours a week. Then, they put the burden entirely on us to repair ourselves on our own time so we can come back for more!'[59]

According to the International Workforce Management Study, September 1998,[60] conducted over thirteen countries by the consulting groups Gemini Consulting and Yankelovich Partners, workers worldwide seem to be saying that they want more balance in their lives and are not getting it. This study polled 10,339 workers and found that they want the same things, regardless of country or culture. The study found the five most desired qualities to be:

(1) the ability to balance work and personal life;
(2) work that is truly enjoyable;
(3) security for the future;
(4) good pay or salary;
(5) enjoyable co-workers.

Only in Russia did 'having a good pay or salary' rank higher than 'balancing the needs of work and family/personal life'. Happiest were the French employees; unhappiest were the Japanese. More than half those surveyed did not know their company's mission statement and 84% didn't consider it fundamental to their work. 44% didn't feel connected to their employers.

A survey[61] of more than 800 mid-career executives in the US showed that unhappiness and dissatisfaction are at a 40-year high. Four out of ten interviewed 'hated' what they did. This figure is double that surveyed forty years ago. The same survey showed that nearly half of all Americans would be more satisfied with their lives if they felt they could do more to make a difference in their community.

'There is a growing sense of "dis-spiritedness" in individuals and in the overall workplace. The spirit has been shut down. It can't fully express itself. There is a sense of dis-engagement. It may not be completely quantifiable, but people can and do feel the lack of spirit in their workplace,' comments Martin Rutte.[62]

Corinne McLaughlin says 'Growing numbers of business people want their spirituality to be more than just faith and belief – they want it to be practical and applied. They want to bring their whole selves to work – body, mind and spirit',[63] and leadership and management consultant Donald McCormick[64] notes that 'many believing managers say their relationship with God influences their work lives more than any other factor.' Alan Pritz,[65] highlights that studies on sensitivity to workforce interests have revealed burgeoning employee desire to work for socially responsible, ethically-driven organisations that allow the whole self to be brought to work. 'This in turn,' he says, 'has sparked corporate recognition of the value of promoting personal integration at work; of harnessing not only intellectual capability for peak performance, but emotional and spiritual passion as well.' Dr Ernst Volgenau, founder, president and CEO of the highly successful systems development organisation SRA, is an example of the new thinking at work: he comments that as an engineer, he wanted to set up a company that would use technology to solve societal problems

– that would not just *be a technology* company. He told himself that he would like to have a company that mirrored his interests.[66]

(15) Public opinion

According to a USA Weekend poll held in July 1998[67], spirituality is cited as the second most important factor in personal happiness (after health) by 47% of Americans questioned, and *Business Week*[68] discovered that 95% of Americans reject the idea that a corporation's only purpose is to make money. In November 1995, a *Newsweek* poll[69] reported that 95% of all Americans profess to believe in God, 48% claim they talk about their faith with their associates in the workplace and 78% of Americans feel the need to experience spiritual growth in their lives. The Gallup Organisation, one of the world's largest management and consulting firms,[70] asserts that studies reveal more than half of America's citizens feel they've become 'too busy' with vocational pursuits to 'enjoy God' and give appropriate attention to their spiritual lives, and Professors Tara Fenwick and Elizabeth Lange[71] comment 'People everywhere are searching for a path to wholeness and playfulness – a self-actualised state. There is a renewed hunger to answer basic questions. Is this all there is? What is my life's purpose? How best can I fulfil my purpose? What should I do to live my life well? How do I really experience being alive? The materialism of the 80s has given way to a period of reflectiveness where people are striving to satisfy their hunger for purpose. They need to find wholeness in their lives and their work and their occupations need to be something that fits – fits comfortably into totality of their lives.' In the absence of data from other countries in the West, it is difficult to assess how reflective these statistics are of non-US societies. However, the reference to the work of Dannah Zohar and Ian Marshall made earlier in this chapter strongly indicates that people in consumer cultures *have* become too busy and are indeed aware that their lives are out of kilter.

(16) The proliferation of books, articles, seminars, conferences and websites

'Spirituality is becoming more a part of mainstream society,' says Janice Turner. 'It has been said that one way to measure a society's psyche is to look at the books that sell – and books on religion and spirituality are top sellers in North America.'[72] In fact, bookstores all over the western world are expanding their bookshelves to cope with both the demand for books on spirituality and the increasing number of titles (well over 300 in the past decade). Some of the titles include: *Soul of Business, Liberating the Corporate Soul, Working from the Heart, The Stirring of Soul in the Workplace, Jesus CEO, Spirit at Work, Redefining the Corporate Soul, The Corporate Mystic, Leading with Soul, Take Your Soul to Work, True Work, The Soul's Code, The Reinvention of Work, Care of the Soul, The Politics of Meaning, Leading with Soul, The Ecology of Commerce, Chicken Soup for the Soul at Work, The Global Brain Awakens, Building a Win-Win World, Leadership from the Inside Out,* and, of course, Stephen Covey's *Seven Habits of Highly Effective People* which has sold a multi-millions amount of copies.

Judi Neal, Associate Professor of Management at the University of New Haven, Conneticut, began publishing a quarterly newsletter, Spirit at Work, in 1994. In just under two years, her subscription base grew to more than 1,000 including many human resource and organisational development specialists.

Articles on the subject have spawned. Examples include the cover story in MacLean's magazine, October 1994, entitled 'The New Spirituality: Mainstream North America Searches for Meaning in Life' which documents how people are asking with compelling rigour, traditional questions of philosophy, theology and everyday life as they seek to understand their place in the world; the lead article in the 1 November 1999 *Business Week* magazine entitled 'Religion in the Workplace: The growing presence of spirituality in Corporate America'; an April 2001 edition of *USA Today* which carries a cover story entitled 'Great Minds Reflect on How God Fits Into the Equation' and the main article in a Harvard Business School Bulletin.

There are currently over 20,000 websites on the subject 'Spirituality'.

There were over twenty conferences in 1999 in Canada and the US alone on the theme of 'Spirituality in the Workplace', including in the same year one hosted by the prestigious American Management Association on 'Profiting from a Values-Based Culture', which focused on how to tap into the fourth dimension of spirituality and ethics as crucial components for success. Since the late 1980s, the University of Sheffield in England has pondered the subject, beginning with its 1988 conference on 'Spirituality in Organisations' and since 1998, the Rural Resource Development Agency in County Clare, Ireland, has been running its conference 'Our Society in the New Millennium' which has focused on re-appraising the values governing Irish life, shaping the kind of Ireland we want to experience, creating work-life balance, redefining roles and relationships, spirituality at work, love at work among many other related topics. The Irish Institute for Training and Development hosts an annual national conference. In 1998, one of the topics was spirituality at work. The Chrysallis Centre in County Wicklow, Ireland, offers conferences and seminars on the practical aspects of spirituality. In 1999, at Davos, Switzerland, the World Economic Forum offered topics such as 'Spiritual Anchors for the New Millennium' and 'The Future of Meditation in a Networked Economy'. The 1998 International Conference on Business and Consciousness held in November at the Mexican resort of Puerto Vallarta heard how the giant consulting firm McKinsey and Co. was using spiritually-based training techniques to boost clients' productivity and profits.

There are many training programmes and seminars dealing with the subject: 30 MBA Programmes in the US now offer courses; the University of Trento, Italy, offers the subject

'Spirituality in the Workplace'. The 1996 Industry Report[73] issued by *Training Magazine* shows that 37% of US companies provide training in ethics and 68% in personal growth. Increasingly, personal growth programmes in business human resource development are presenting explicitly spiritual material including fostering social and spiritual transformation in the workplace: the further development of human consciousness through spiritual understanding and MentorMedia's 'Character-Building' programme fostering personal integrity and the development of 'good' character including 'good' values, self-control and the ability to do the 'right' thing.

Heather Skelton is president of AliveWorks – a company dedicated to helping people identify and develop their passion in life. Heather asks the question 'What does it [the books, articles, conferences and seminars on spirituality at work] mean? Have we now reached that point in global consciousness where we are ready to tackle the biggest transformation of all – bringing consciousness to business and government? And if that is the task at hand, what is our individual role in it?'[74]

(17) Increase in interest in Eastern philosophies

In the West, Intellectual Quotient (IQ) has been the main tool used to analyse and deal with all work issues – even though there is a strong, talented psychology base in the West and Christian Scriptures are rich with thought-provoking answers. Yet in western business, psychology and the truths to be found in the messages of Jesus have been buried under the mountain of IQ so that their truths have not always been available to the searching heart. Many issues defy pure logic. For example, why does a shift of employees not have their workstation clean and ready for the next shift? Why do some employees allow a fault in a product to pass from their stage of production to the next, creating cumulative problems and an unnecessary scrap product? Or why does an employee take a notion and 'call in sick'? These questions can only be answered by using our Emotional Quotient (EQ) and Spiritual Quotient (SQ). Therefore, given that western trust in logic has stifled the support that has been there all along in psychology and Christian spirituality, those looking for answers to the questions logic cannot fathom, turn to Eastern philosophies. These address the mind-heart-spirit connection. *HR Magazine*[75] writes that 'Many business people are growing away from the idea that science and technology can solve every business problem. Philosophies like Zen Buddhism, Confucianism and Shintoism tend to emphasise values such as loyalty to one's group and the ability to find a spiritual "centre" in any kind of work or activity.' And Lee Bolman,[76] Professor of Leadership at the University of Missouri, Kansas City, says there is a great deal of fascination with Eastern philosophies among both his students and the corporate clients he counsels.

(18) Advances in science and health care

The research of Neuropsychologist Michael Persinger and Neurologist V.S Ramachandran[77] has proven that there is a 'God Spot' in the frontal lobe area of the brain. In much the same way that a novice might ask what a particular socket at the back of a computer is for, so these scientists are posing this question: if there is nothing to connect to, then why do we have this equipment? Just as these scientists have been able to point to the bundles of neural networks that comprise the emotional intelligence, which psychologist and award-winning writer Dan Goleman[78] has discussed so thoroughly in his book, so we now have a scientific basis to discuss the generic concept of spirituality as part of our 'equipment' as opposed to it being the domain of this or that religion.

The research findings of three other scientists[79] prove that our 'equipment' is designed to explore the deeper issues of life. The work of Austrian neurologist Wolf Singer in the 1990s has shown that there is a neural process in the brain devoted to unifying and giving meaning to our experience. The work of Professor Rodolfo Llinas of New York University School of Medicine in the mid 1990s using enhanced new magneto-encephalographic (MEG) technology allows whole-skull studies of the brain's oscillating electrical fields and their associated magnetic fields and thus, visually describes Singer's findings. Harvard neurologist and biological anthropologist, Terrance Deacon, published findings in 1997[80] that 'show that language is a uniquely human activity... that co-evolved with rapid development in the brain's frontal lobes' and that 'neither existing computers nor even higher apes (with rare and limited exception) can use language, because they lack the frontal lobe facility for dealing with meaning...'. Deacon's neurobiological work on language and symbolic representation shows that 'we have used SQ (Spiritual Intelligence) literally to grow our human brains. SQ has 'wired' us to become the people we are and gives us the potential for further 'rewiring' – for growth and transformation, for further evolution of our human potential...creativity, flexibility and vision.'[81]

Research and discoveries in quantum theory have moved understanding away from the old sixteenth-century Newtonian model of the world, in which all that exists is what can be seen and as such, everything and everyone is separate, to the fact that 'everything substantial is insubstantial';[82] 'we live in an intelligent universe... and this intelligent universe brings to us the realities that match our belief systems';[83] 'electrons store thought and communicate with one another irrespective of time and distance', i.e. we have the equivalent of a 'thought internet'.[84] So, instead of thinking that we are isolated from everyone and everything, that we are the victims of large forces on the earth and that there is a sharp split between the observer and the observed, i.e. my thoughts do not affect reality (the view given to mankind by the Newtonian model), we now know (from the quantum theory model) that we are all part of a sea of atomic energy and while each person and circumstance

seems separate, they are in fact like a wave on that sea; we now
know that we are, therefore, all interconnected and, most
importantly of all, that our own thoughts or the collective
thinking of our environment or our culture are creating the
realities that we are experiencing. As Einstein said: 'The world
we have created is a product of our way of thinking.' This
knowledge, promulgated in the public domain so eloquently
and powerfully by writer and endocrinologist Dr Deepak
Chopra[85] and biologist and author Rupert Sheldrake[86] has
sparked in organisations the realisation that they must ground
their leadership and employees in this 'new' understanding of
how the world works and has sparked in the large numbers of
the public the need to educate themselves as to how to use their
'thought' equipment effectively so that they produce creative
and not destructive results. Hence, the huge array of subliminal
and paraliminal tapes, self-help books and tools. Scientists in
other disciplines, too, have had to face the facts posed by
quantum theory and, in particular, Werner Heisenberg's
'uncertainty principle' (the main tenet of quantum theory) that
we can only know the aspect of reality that we are looking for;
our answers will always be answers only to the questions that
we ask; truth depends on our point of view. So, we now see the
need for intuition, meditation, creativity to stretch people out
of the limitations of their current thinking. Because, as
Heisenberg says, quantum reality itself is filled with infinite
realities, we now also see that while 'things' can sometimes
look bleak, there is an infinite array of possibilities because
reality is only limited to what our thoughts can imagine. This
truth has meant that political leaders are exploring[87] how to
change the thinking of their peoples so that the collective
thinking of those peoples creates a reality that is supportive of
the shared values of the nation.

Dr Candace Pert is a pharmacologist and researcher on
emotions and health. Dr Pert[88] has strengthened the voice of
quantum theory. Her research shows that every time we think

a thought, our brain releases the brain chemical equivalent to that thought. Dr Pert also discovered that neurotransmitters, which are attached to each molecule of the body, eavesdrop on the brain to find out what chemical is being released and then themselves release that chemical in every molecule. So, if someone feels life is awful/people are awful, the brain will release a chemical commensurate with that thought and flood the body with that not so nice chemistry! In other words, Dr Pert's work has proven that the human being is responsible for his/her own internal climate. Hence the huge number of books and seminars on 'choosing how to respond' to life, managing one's thoughts and change-management programmes that begin with the individual.

Developments in health care have encouraged the 'journey within'. Co-dependancy experts such as Melody Beattie[89] offer 'recovery' programmes, books, tapes and videos which encourage the individual to let go, on a deep level, their need to be victimised and to be victims. 'We need to let go of our need to be in dysfunctional relationships and systems at work, in love in family relationships, in friendships. We deserve better. It is our right. When we believe in our right to happiness, we will have happiness. We will fight for that right and the right will emerge from our souls. Break free from oppression and victimisation.' This is one reason why so many have chosen to leave organisations that do not have healthy work practices and values and move to those that do.

Building on the 1975 pioneering work of Dr Herbert Benson,[90] a Harvard cardiologist who demonstrated (and still does) that certain meditation practices produce a relaxation effect that reduces blood pressure without medicinal agents, the Institute of Heartmath offers a variety of de-stress programmes to organisations and, in doing so, gives the employee the legitimate 'go-ahead' to turn his/her attention within to harness the healing power of the mind.

(19) Increasing awareness of natural disasters and the environment

The French economist Georges Anderla, of the Organisation for Economic Cooperation and Development, estimated in 1973 that humanity was doubling its knowledge every six years. By 1990, Dr Jacques Valee estimated that global knowledge was doubling every 18 months.[91] Some of that knowledge centres on the increasing incidence of natural disasters. The effects in Europe of the El Nino and El Nina weather systems have been televised, showing thousands of ancient trees destroyed in Paris in 2000 and massive flooding. *Time* magazine[92] documented the severe droughts in Australia caused by El Nino. The devastating effects of hurricanes (Honduras), Tornadoes (America), heavy rains (Africa and India) and earthquakes (India, Guatemala, Peru) have been captured by television on a regular basis. World affairs expert and writer, Hal Lindsey,[93] documents two US Geological Surveys on earthquakes. He reports that from 1890 to 1899, only one killer earthquake (6.0 or more on the Richter Scale) was recorded. From 1990 to 1994, there were more than 100 over 6.0 on the Richter Scale. He reports that in 1996, there were over 10 earthquakes over 6.0 on the Richter scale in February alone. This kind of knowledge has caused people to question how safe the planet is and to think more deeply about what is 'going on' at a global level.

The geologist and spiritual writer, Greg Braden,[94] reminds us that we are at the closing stages of a 200,000-year old cycle at the end of which the magnetic force fields of the earth change: north becomes south and vice versa. (The physical world does not turn upside down! It is the poles that change.) He suggests that on an imaginary scale of ten, we are at position one. He also documents that the collective resonance of all objects on the earth (every object, animate and inanimate, has a sonic resonance) would be a frequency of 13 by the year 2000 (based on the data he had at the time of writing his book). Frequency is measured on a scale called Fibonacci and 13 is the highest rating on that scale. After that, says Braden, we move out of this three-dimensional sphere into the fourth dimension. He reminds the reader that the Kings Chamber in the Great Pyramid was created to resonate with a 13 frequency precisely because it was thought that this frequency would usher the pharaoh into the spiritual realm. So, says Braden, the whole planet is effectively sending out a signal: 'Return to the Spirit'.

It is interesting that physicist and systems theorist Fritjof Capra[95] wrote: 'When the concept of human spirit is understood as the mode of consciousness in which the individual feels connected to the cosmos as a whole, it becomes clear that ecological awareness is spiritual in its deepest sense.'

(20) Pressures of modern society are leading us into the 'sixth extinction'

According to Paleoanthropologist Richard Leakey,[96] the pressures of modern society are leading us into the 'sixth extinction'. For the first time in history, he says, we are experiencing the environmental impact of economic activity and human population at a global level. Some environmentalists believe that the burden of pollution is rapidly reaching a point where it will destabilise the world's food chains and ecosystems.[97] The Science Council of Japan states clearly that

> If the industrialised countries continue with lifestyles of mass production, mass consumption and mass wastage, then the underlying supply of resources, energy and foodstuffs will inevitably start dwindling rapidly by the middle of the 21st century at the latest. In addition to the finite limits of resources, the earth and human society are starting to reach their limits with respect to the ability to absorb waste and harmful substances. The combination of finite resources and natural limitations, together with the rate of acceleration in the world

population, will cause a catastrophe which will rapidly erode the prosperity and well-being of the industrialised countries. Indeed, the second half of the 21st Century holds the prospect of a new chapter in the tragedy of mankind, one from which the human race cannot escape...The industrialised nations, with their international influence, must now espouse far-sighted ideals based on resolute principles and take concrete action to save the earth, nature and the human race. If not, it is clear that the "compound devastation spiral" will accelerate and human civilisation will be in danger of extinction by the second half of the 21st Century.[98]

(21) We are in a different type of age

'The major issue on people's minds today is meaning,' say Danah Zohar and Ian Marshall, 'it isn't enough for people to find happiness within their existing framework. They want to question the framework itself, to question the value of how they are living their lives and to find new value, that elusive "more". Just by asking such questions, they are showing a need to use their spiritual intelligence.'[99]

Twenty per cent of the world's population – that is, those living in the industrialised world – have experienced an unprecedented level of material well-being. Yet, they feel they are lacking something, that there is an emptiness to be filled and those who have looked to formal religion to fill that emptiness have discovered that it is not able to fill it. Modern western society has thrown away many factors that gave life meaning: tradition, community, God, moral codes and replaced them with an 'anything-goes' framework for living in which we can take very little for granted. Consequently, we have issues, complexities and questions that our forbears would neither have faced or raised.

Quantum theory has given us a new way of looking at life: the observer and the observed are connected; we see what we expect to see. Therefore, modern man knows s/he can expect to see a variety of experiences and so s/he asks 'what are the many things I might see?', 'What is possible?' So, modern man is slowly moving out of 'rut' thinking (as Deepak Chopra says 'bondage is thinking with a limited range of possibilities'[100]) into possibility thinking by questioning. This has become the *modus operandi* of our times.

Author Thomas Moore[101] writes: 'The great malady of the twentieth century, implicated in all of our troubles and affecting us, individually and socially, is "loss of soul".' When soul is neglected, it doesn't just go away; it appears symptomatically in obsessions, addictions, violence and loss of meaning. Our temptation is to isolate these symptoms or to try to eradicate them one by one; but the root problem is that we have lost our wisdom about the soul, even our interest in it. Education professors Tara Fenwick and Elizabeth Lang of the University of Alberta comment that

> This spiritual search seems to have become more urgent in the late 20th Century when pervasive dissatisfaction and even despair have been produced by an age centred on appetite and material consumption... [one critic] contends that modernity's economic universalism, aggressive realism and rugged individualism have created an age of narcissism wherein lonely people pursue empty hyperactivity. Slattery (1995) writes that people are fed up with materialistic self-gratification, shallow individualism, militaristic competitiveness, rampant over-consumption and pandering paternalism fed them by the media and marketplace in an orgy of technological splendour. It is no wonder that people are searching for meaning as well as personal healing, wholeness, peace, joy and connectedness.[102]

Fenwick and Lange also talk of the new knowledge and learning demands that have been created by an ever increasing amount of information, accelerated competition and technological advances which are shortening time and shrinking space. For example, some executives receive many hundreds of emails each day, global competition requires constant re-skilling and knowledge updates, mobile and satellite telephones facilitate fast access and response while digital cameras and robotics allow for inputs to a production process from team members spread across many geographic sites.

Technology is dictating the pace of twenty-first century living and the consumer culture is ensuring that people buy the products that use the technology. Flexibility, not stability, is the anthem for the contemporary organisation as it strives to remain competitive in an increasingly tough global market. So, employees are expected to be flexible, quick-learning, innovative, supportive members of self-governing teams which are formed to meet fast-changing organisational needs. When these needs have been met, the teams are dissolved and reformed in a new grouping to meet a new need. This lack of stability can be anxiety-laden if employees are not taught how to emotionally cope with constant change. The more conditions of anxiety are created, the more fervently people seek a quiet space for balance.

Peter Vaill[103] speaks of the fact that it is difficult for employees to have the loyalty to their companies that employees had in the past because of leveraged buy-outs which see organisations as mere asset pools to be plundered. He also speaks of the tremendous flux in organisations today where fixity is gone in favour of rapid turnover of product, people and leaders. This has meant that people do not get the time to build up allegiances to 'wise, reassuring and charismatic leaders'. He shows concern over the multiplicity of increasingly powerful stakeholders in today's organisation with competing, even contradictory claims on the organisation making it very difficult to commit to one mission. He also comments on the fact that organisations have to regularly reinvent themselves and leaders correspondingly must go through profound personal transformations, involving physical and mental health and their family relationships.

Humanistic psychologist Abraham Maslow created the famous pyramid of 'Man's Hierarchy of Needs'. In this, he declares that self-actualisation (the highest need) is a state sought by all human beings once they have satisfied their more basic needs of survival, gratification and belonging. It would seem that our consumer society has given us all it can in meeting these basic needs and that its fear-laden shortcomings and the environmental dangers it has created have driven western man to explore how s/he can meet that highest need.

(22) The new corporate evolutionary imperative

Clearly, from what I have documented above, business has become the most powerful force in society. This means that if social and environmental problems are to be solved, business must accept a leadership role (as the Japanese Science Council points out). It will take time for business to be fully comfortable with this new role.

A global economy means doing business with different cultures. Not all cultures operate on the same premise as do western cultures. Asian cultures, for example, have business networks that favour doing business with their own culture instead of doing business with someone from a different culture. The issue here is about sharing values. Fukuyama points this out and highlights that conflict is not likely to be based on political persuasion but around cultural persuasion: western, Islamic, Confucian, Japanese, Hindu and so on. Social collaboration is important for any economic activity to function effectively. In a global economic activity social collaboration must be found across all cultures. But cooperation requires good personal and interpersonal skills (IQ and EQ). However, to transcend cultural barriers, the only part of the person capable of doing this is his/her spiritual centre, his/her spiritual intelligence (SQ) Hence, it is more likely, according to Fukuyama, 'that a successful market economy, rather than being the cause of stable democracy, is co-determined by the prior factor of social capital' and this 'makes clear why capitalism and democracy are so closely related.'[104] So, another role of business is to ensure democracy via healthy social capital which in its cross-cultural form can only be achieved by connecting people to their spiritual centre.

Notes

1.   Corinne McLaughlin, 'Spirituality in the Workplace', 1999, www.walkerinternational.com/article63.html

2.   'Spirituality in Corporations', www.reemcreatoins.com/literature/corporations.html

3.   National Speakers Bureau, 'Spirituality in the Workplace,' First filed 18/12/00 www.nsb.com/whatsnew.asp?I_newsid=146

4.   Peter Grazier, 'The Toxic Workplace', www.teambuildinginc.com/article_toxic.htm

5.   Joseph Jaworski, *Synchronicity* (San Francisco, CA: Berrett-Koehler, 1996). p. 64

6.   OECD, 2000 Development Co-operation Report

7.   Danah Zohar and Ian Marshall, *SQ: Connecting with our Spiritual Intelligenc* (NY: Bloomsbury Publishing, 2000), p. 16

8.   Ian I. Mitroff & Elizabeth Denton, *A Spiritual Audit of Corporate America* (San Francisco, CA: Jossey-Bass Inc. Pub., 1999) Foreword by Warren Bennis, University of Southern California, p. xi

9.   Peter B. Vaill, *Spirited Leading And Learning* (San Francisco, CA: Jossey-Bass, 1998), p. 179

10.   Richard Barrett, *Liberating the Corporate Soul* (USA: Butterworth-Heinemann, 1998). p. 147

11.   M. U. Hart, *Working and educating for Life: Feminist and international perspectives on adult education* (NY: Routledge 1992) p. 87

12.   Grazier, 'The Toxic Workplace'

13.   The Science Council of Japan, 'Towards a Comprehensive Solution to Problems in Education and the Environment based on a Recognition of Human Dignity and Self-Worth,' July, 2000

14. Frederick G. Harmon, *Playing for Keeps* (New York: John Wiley & Sons, 1996), pp. 4-5
15. Francis Fukuyama, *Trust: The Social Virtues And The Creation of Prosperity* (London: Hamish Hamilton Ltd., 1995). pp. 13-19
16. Vaill, op. cit., p. 192
17. Robert K Greenleaf, *The Power of Servant Leadership*, edited by Larry C Spears (San Francisco: Berrett-Koehler Publishers, Inc., 1998), Advance praise, James A. Autry
18. Jeffrey Pfeffer, *The Human Equation* (Boston: Harvard Business School Press, 1998), p. 137
19. Ann Coombs, *The Living Workplace* (Warwick Publications, 2001) & www.nsb.com/whatsnew.asp?j_newsid=146
20. Alan L.Pritz, www.innerresourceenhancement.com/spirituality_workplace.htm
21. Hans Selye, *Stress Without Distress* (London: Corgi, 1987)
22. Cheryl C Belles, 'Spirituality as a Subtle Change Force (Part II) www.consultativecoaching.com/ezines/mar_2001.htm
23. Barrett, op. cit. pp. 144-145
24. Zohar and Marshall, op. cit., pp. 199-200
25. Fukuyama, op. cit., p. 7
26. Corinne McLaughlin, 'Spirituality in the Workplace', 1999, www.walkerinternational.com/article63.html
27. Ibid.
28. Lewis Richmond, *Work as a Spiritual Practice* (Bantum Doubleday Dell Pub, 2000)
29. The Cone/Roper Cause-Related Trends Report, 1999, www.roper.com/Newsroom/content/news115.htm
30. Barrett, p. 32
31. Corinne McLaughlin, World Goodwill Occasional Paper, April 1999
32. Marci McDonald, 'Shush the Guy in the Cubicle is Mediating,' *Business & Technology* 05/03/99 www.usnews.com/usnews/issue/990503/3spir.htm
33. Alan L. Pritz, 'Spirituality in the Workplace: A New Dynamic', www.innerresourceenhancement.com/spirituality_workplace.htm
34. Abe McLaughlin, 'Seeking Spirituality... At Work', *The Christian Science Monitor* 16 March 1998 Edition, www.csmonitor.com/durable/1998/03/16/us/us.2.html

35.   Martin Rutte, 'Spirituality in the Workplace',
      www.martinrutte.com/heart.html
36.   Alfie Kohn 'Challenging Behaviorist Dogma: Myths About Money
      and Motivation', *Compensation and Benefits Review*, 1998
37.   Robert Quinn, *Change the World* (San Francisco: Jossey-Bass Inc.,
      Pub., 2000), p xviii
38.   Jaworski, op. cit., pp. 8-11
39.   James Joyce, *Portrait of the Artist as a Young Man* (Vintage Books, 1993)
40.   Mitroff and Denton, op. cit., p. xiii
41.   Martin Rutte, 'Spirituality in the Workplace',
      www.martinrutte.com/heart.html
42.   Richard Barrett,
      www.fastcompany.com/online/16/barrett.html
43.   Harmon, op. cit., p. 3
44.   Fukuyama, op. cit., p. 4
45.   Mitroff and Denton, op. cit., cover
46.   Robert Levering & Milton Moskowitz, *The 100 Best Companies to
      Work for in America* (New York: Doubleday, 1993)
47.   Anthony Rucci, Stephen P. Kim and Richard T. Quinn, 'The
      Employee-Customer-Profit Chain at Sears', *Harvard Business
      Review*, January-February 1998, pp. 82-97
48.   Ibid.
49.   *Business Week*, November 1, 1999
50.   For a free copy of the survey call William M. Mercer + (1) 502 561-
      4759 www.wmmercer.com
51.   Michael Cox and Michael E. Rock, *Seven Pillars of Leadership*
      (Toronto: Dryden, 1997), pp. 10-13
52.   Linda Grant, 'Happy Workers, High Returns,' *Fortune Magazine*,
      January 1998, p. 8
53.   Michele Hunt, *Dream Makers* (Palo Alto, CA: Davies-Black
      Publishing, 1998), p. 70
54.   David C. Trott, Fluor Daniel: 'Results of Spiritual Well-being
      Study', Department of Education Administration, The University
      of Austin, Texas, 1995
55.   'Study of Business Performance, Employee Satisfaction, and
      Leadership', Wilson Learning Corporation
56.   Wayne Jackson, 'The Christian And The Workplace',
      www.christiancourier.com/penpoints/workplace.htm
57.   Corinne McLaughlin, 1999
      www.walkerinternational.com/article63.html

58. Kay Bird, 'Bringing Spirituality Into The Workplace', www.martinrutte.com/reporter.html
59. Mitroff and Denton, op. cit., p. 4
60. International Workforce Management Study, September 1998. www.gemcon.com
61. Richard Merlin, *Washington Post*, August 25 1996, reporting on a survey by Joy Schneer of Rider University and Frieda Reitman of Pace University
62. Martin Rutte, 'Spirituality In The Workplace', www.martinrutte.com/heart.html
63. Corinne McLaughlin www.walkerinternational.com/article63.html
64. Donald W. McCormick, 'Spirituality and Management' www.newton.uor.edu/FacultyFolder/DmcCormick/Spirituality.html
65. Alan L.Pritz, www.innerresourceenhancement.com/spirituality_workplace.htm
66. Hunt, op. cit., p.16
67. *USA Weekend* Poll, July 1998
68. Corinne McLaughlin, World Goodwill Occasional Paper, April 1999
69. Wayne Jackson, 'The Christian And The Workplace' www.christiancourier.com/penpoints/workplace.htm
70. George Gallup and Timothy Jones, *The Next American Spirituality: Finding God in the Twenty-First Century* (Colorado Springs, CO: Cook, 2000), p.191
71. Tara Fenwick and Elizabeth Lange, www.ualberta.ca/~tfenwick/ext/spirit.htm
72. Janice Turner, 'Spirituality in the Workplace'. *An organization can really benefit when it provides a humanistic environment where employees can reach their highest potential* www.camagazine.com/camagazine.nsf/e1999-dec/Ethics
73. *Training Magazine*, 1996 Industry Report
74. Heather Skelton, 'Spirituality in the Workplace' www.omegactr.com/source/spirwork.htm
75. Ellen Brandt, 'Corporate Pioneers Explore Spirituality' www.shrm.org/hrmagazine/articles/0496spir.htm
76. Ibid.
77. Zohar and Marshall, op. cit., p. 11
78. Daniel Goleman, *Emotional Intelligence* (London: Bloomsbury Publishing Plc., 1996)
79. Michael Persinger, *Neuropsychological Bases of God Beliefs* (Praeger

Pub: 1999); W Singer, 'Striving for Coherence', C. M. Gray & W. Singer, 'Stimulus-Specific Neuronal Oscillations in Orientation Columns of Cat Visual Cortex' & 'Visual Feature Integration and the Temporal Correlation Hypothesis'& Vilayanur Ramachandran & Sandra Blakeslee, *Phantoms in the Brain: Probing the Mysteries in the Human Mind* (William Morrow & Co., 1998), see also www.wired.com, www.cseti.org, www.cas.bellarmine.edu/tietjen/images/new_page_2.htm & www.abcnews.go.com/sections/living/SecondOpinion/

80.   Terrance Deacon, *The Symbolic Species: The Evolution of Language and the Brain* (W. W. Nortan & Co., 1997)

81.   Zohar and Marshall, op. cit., pp. 12-13

82.   Jaworski, op. cit., p. 177

83.   Rupert Sheldrake, www.sheldrake.org

84.   Ibid.

85.   Deepak Chopra, New Physics of Healing [Audio Cassette] (Boulder, CO: Sounds True Recordings, 1990); *Magical Mind Magical Body* (Nighingate Conant Corp.) Tape 1 & 6

86.   Rupert Sheldrake, *The Presence of the Past: Morphic Resonance and the Habits of Nature* (Inner Traditions Intl. Ltd, 1995)

87.   Jaworski, op. cit., p.140; www.chopra.com

88.   Candace B. Pert, *Molecules of Emotion* (London: Simon and Schuster, 1998)

89.   Melody Beattie, *The Language of Letting Go* (Center City, MN: Hazelden, 1990), p. 36

90.   Herbert Benson, *The Relaxation Response* (London: Collins, 1976); Alan L Pritz, 'Spirituality in the Workplace: A New Dynamic', www.innerresourceenhancement.com/spirituality_workplace.htm

91.   Peter Russell, *The White Hold in the Time* (San Francisco: Harper 1992) p. 28

92.   *Time Magazine*, 31 Jan. 2000, 27 Sept. 1999, 27 July 1998 and 18 Aug. 1997

93.   Hal Lindsey, *Planet Earth 2000 AD* (CA: Western Front Ltd, 1994), p. 85

94.   Gregg Braden, *Awakening to Zero Point* (Bellevue, Washington: Radio Bookstore, 1997)

95.   Fritjof Capra, *The Web of Life: A New Understanding of Living Systems* (Doubleday, 1997)

96.   Richard Leakey and Roger Lewin, *Origins Reconsidered* (New York: Doubleday, 1992), p. 353

97. World Resources Institute in collaboration with the United Nations Environment Programme and the United Nations Development Programme, *World Resources: A Guide to the Global Environment 1994-95* (New York: Oxford University Press, 1994), pp. 213-214
98. The Science Council of Japan
99. Zohar and Marshall, op. cit., p. 8
100. Deepak Chopra (1990), op. cit.
101. Thomas Moore, *Care of the Soul: A Guide for Cultivating Death and Sacredness in Everyday Life* (HarperPerennial Library, 1994)
102. Tara Fenwick and Elizabeth Lange, www.ualberta.ca/~tfenwick/ext/spirit.htm
103. Vaill, op. cit., p. 175
104. Fukuyama, op. cit., p. 356

CHAPTER II

WHAT EXACTLY IS SPIRITUAL INTELLIGENCE IN THE WORKPLACE?

Your vision will become clear only when you look into your heart.
Who looks outside, dreams; who looks inside, awakens.
– Carl Jung

Spiritual intelligence in the workplace can be discussed under eleven broad headings: *Spirituality does not mean religion, Spiritual intelligence, Quantum theory and psychoneuroimmunology, General characteristics, Personal characteristics, The work environment internally supportive of spirituality, The work environment externally supportive of spirituality, National/political aspects, Specific techniques, Research* and *Obstacles.*

Let's take a closer look at each of these eleven categories:

(1) Spirituality does not mean religion

It would seem, from those who have written about this subject, that there is a vast difference between spirituality and religion.

Religion is considered to consist of beliefs, rules, structure and tradition, and connecting to the Divine via the latter. Spirituality is about the inner journey – perhaps the journey of the Prodigal – and as such it is seen as an experience, a highly personal experience. But each person's experience can be different and, therefore, their journeys will differ. However, underpinning each journey are two common threads: experiences that result in a sloughing off of an aspect of the ego that invariably the individual did not realise was there; and the learning of a set of principles during the course of this cleansing process, usually in the form of one principle being discovered as that part of the ego which 'covered' the principle is removed.

Because of these two common threads, those who are well on their inner 'journey' can act as a mentor for those just embarking or those not quite as far along. One of the key principles to be discovered along this journey is that fear exists and can be conquered by love. Fear is experienced via a constant set of experiences which trigger in the individual all the subsets of fear, beginning with doubt, then worry, anxiety, catastrophic thinking, then fear itself and the aftermath of fear: destructiveness, negativity and conditional love. The individual is challenged to respond to fear and its elements with Trust in Divine Love, courage, goodwill, anastrophic thinking (the opposite of catastrophic thinking), constructiveness and unconditional love, knowing that if s/he does this, then a force greater than the individual will be triggered to move on his/her behalf either within or outside the individual. For some, this force is Divine Intelligence; for others the Source; for yet others the Universe; for still others the 'unified field' in quantum physics, and for others – God. This process of facing fear with trust in Love is very similar to the process the Egyptians imagined their dead Pharaohs experienced. To facilitate the process, the Egyptians built three chambers in a pyramid representing the three stages of spiritual evolution before entering Heaven. The first of these chambers, the Initiate's

Chamber, 'is the chamber specially designed to force the 'battle' between fear and trust in Love in the Pharaoh.[1]

The net effect of undergoing such a spiritual experience is threefold: firstly, the individual experiences enormous liberation and a sense of being empowered as a result of conquering his/her fears and the force of Fear; secondly, the individual begins to discover talents which s/he did not realise s/he had because these talents were being strangled by the hold of Fear; and thirdly, the individual begins to display a different character – a character resplendent with love, joy, peace, patience, kindness, goodness, gentleness, faithfulness and self-control. What St Paul called the 'fruits of the Spirit'.[2] In this regard, spirituality is seen as radically different to religion, in that anyone can be religious by subscribing to a set of rules, traditions, ceremonies and reading from the writings of the scriptures of one's tradition. In contrast, it takes courage, commitment to the journey, tenacity to continue through the inevitable dark periods of the journey, trust in the face of apparent defeat, and discipline to allow the process of ego to be dismantled and the Spirit of Love to shine through. The importance of this releasing of character qualities is underscored by the Dalai Lama who wrote: 'Religion is something we can perhaps do without. What we can't do without are those basic spiritual qualities such as love and compassion, patience, tolerance, forgiveness, contentment, a sense of responsibility, a sense of harmony.'[3]

Spirituality is seen as a 'leveller' of people because it is non-denominational, inclusive, universal and allows for diversity of expression. It also emphasises the application of itself to the everyday, to the moment. Religion is seen as divisive in that in requires compliance with a certain set of traditions/ceremonies/dogmas as opposed to the release of the spirit-character or 'fruits of the Spirit' as described above. Religion is also seen as a once a week affair, unrelated to the everyday or the moment. For these reasons, religion has been almost outlawed in the workplace, which has traditionally experienced enough divisions across functions never mind having to cope with yet another reason for division. In their *Spiritual Audit of Corporate America,* Ian Mitroff and Elizabeth Denton[4] discovered that some people were so concerned about the concept of spirituality because of the religious connotations of division and conflict, that they were afraid to even use the words 'spirituality' and 'soul'. However, the majority of those they studied felt that this sensitive nettle should be grasped and the words should be used. Otherwise we would slump into a 'moral relativism' as in, for example 'all values are equally good unless they hurt someone.'

Spirituality is also seen as more of a question than a definitive answer: it is the process of inquiry that generates depth, clarity and richness of response because there are so many ways of experiencing 'the journey'; it is a process of inquiry also because there are times when logic just does not have the answer and it is only the deep, spiritual search that can lead the individual to that answer.

Spirituality has been expressed in the workplace as a set of shared values, rules and behaviours, and in this regard it is similar to religion, but not as limiting, because instead of these being used to ensure adherence to an institution, they are designed to empower the individual, facilitate his/her spiritual (character) growth in an everyday, applied context.
So, spirituality in the workplace has a much broader feel to it than religion: it addresses more of the factors that are common denominators across humanity and, therefore, it has a unifying effect.

(2) Spiritual intelligence

Much of our lives up to the age of about 23 is forcibly governed by the level of our Intelligence Quotient (IQ): school grades, study, entry into university or college, applications for a job, and so on. In Ireland up until two years ago, so strong was this focus that extra points were given to a student who sat 'Higher Maths' for the Leaving Certificate Standard (the last exams given to students before leaving secondary school). Research on the brain[5] has shown that IQ is a very limited part of the complete brain function, is based on serial neural wiring, and is secondary to our Emotional Quotient (EQ). IQ is interested in rules and, therefore, low IQ makes it impossible for the human to solve rational problems. Emotional Quotient (EQ) is a more advanced and deeper process. It is considered the primary process of the brain as it is connected to deep-seated cultural conditioning which gives the human their affinities, values and dislikes.

Emotional Intelligence is based on associative neural wiring – a much more complex interaction than IQ – which consists of thousands of neural connectors interacting on an ad hoc basis. EQ finds itself in a situation or with someone and uses its vast store of cultural programming (involving images, relationships, patterns, symbols and archetypes) to decide how it should respond in that situation or to that person. Obviously, low EQ would mean that an individual would be socially inept, awkward in any situation with any person and apt to put their proverbial 'foot in it'! Francis Fukuyama[6] casts a very interesting light on the economic and political importance of addressing the EQ element of the brain when he talks of the different cultural norms used in Asia and the US to do business. Asians support one another in a network of business and social links (known as *keiretsu*). Americans prefer the approach that benefits the individual as opposed to the approach that looks for the benefit of the whole. 'Accordingly,' says Fukuyama, 'conflict is likely to arise not among fascism, socialism and democracy, but among the world's major cultural groups: Western, Islamic, Confucian, Japanese, Hindu and so on.' Clearly, if economic (and any other) conflict is to be avoided, work must be done to help nations move from their cultural conditioning – EQ – to a deeper, more universal element of their brain: their Spiritual Quotient. The current conflicts in our world and the terrorist attack on the World Trade Centre and Pentagon in the US demonstrate how urgently education is needed to move humanity from this culturally-bound Emotional Quotient, with its tribal concepts, feelings and bigotries, to its deeper Spiritual Quotient where each member of the human race realises the common denominators s/he shares with other members as well as their oneness.

In terms of activity, it may seem that both IQ and EQ are functioning entirely separately. This is not the case (although in some people, we may think that it is!). In fact, both intelligences work together synergistically so that the sum intelligence is greater than that of the individual two.

Spiritual Quotient (SQ) comprises oscillations moving across the brain at a count of 40 Hz per second. Studies of these oscillations show that the oscillations provide meaning to the outputs of both IQ and EQ, setting them in a context and giving them a value; they are also 'the centre of the self, the neurological sources from which 'I' emerges.'[7] SQ is that part of the individual that enables him/her to see the consequences of his/her action, create a purpose for their lives, change boundaries, ask 'why' of a particular rule and create the possibility of having meaning in their life. So, low SQ means that the individual will make so many errors of judgement that those they deal with are constantly 'mopping up after them'; that the individual has no sense of their true self, value or purpose; and that the data that his/her IQ and EQ are providing are completely lost on the individual.

Closely associated with SQ (i.e. the 40Hz neural oscillations) is the discovery of the 'God Spot' in the brain. Researched by neuropsychologist Michael Persinger in the early 1990s and discovered by neurologist V. S. Ramachandran and his team at the University of California in 1997, the God Spot is an isolated module of neural connections in the temporal lobe areas of the brain. This spot, when activated, gives the individual distinct mystical experiences. However, just as IQ and EQ must be integrated by SQ to give them meaning, the same is true for the God Spot. We may have mystical experiences, but this does not mean that our character will change or that we will be able to change our value system and behaviour as a result, i.e. that we will become more spiritual. Only the 40Hz oscillations (SQ) can confer these results on a God Spot activity. 'The special insights and abilities conferred by the God Spot must be woven into the general fabric of our emotions, motivations and potential and brought into dialogue with the centre of the self and its special way of knowing.'[8] This is why we meet religious people – experiencing God Spot activity – who are low on SQ and why people high on SQ may not be religious: 'Many humanists and atheists have very high SQ; many actively and vociferously religious people have very low SQ... A person high in SQ might practise any religion but without narrowness, exclusiveness, bigotry or prejudice.... SQ is... the intelligence with which we not only recognise existing values, but with which we creatively discover new values.... SQ is not culture-dependent or value-dependent. It does not follow from existing values, but rather creates the very possibility of having values in the first place.'[9] So, high SQ is related to the creation of values and the existence of creativity in an organisation. Since values are the binding agent for human productivity and loyalty, and creativity is the elixir that triggers new products and better ways of doing what we do, high SQ is obviously essential in today's workplace.

The 40Hz oscillations connect the individual to an indwelling centre that is itself connected to the Source. This is a place of deep peace and solitude, a place in which we feel at one with the unified field discovered by quantum physicists, a place that connects the individual to all humanity and life; a place where the individual realises that whatever s/he does to another expression of Life – e.g. human, animal, plant – s/he is doing to himself.

(3) Quantum theory and psychoneuroimmunology

Since 1990, the work of quantum physicists David Bohm, Stephen Hawking and Francisco Varela has been popularised by the seminars, conferences and books of physicist and Medical Doctor Deepak Chopra.[10] Speaking and writing in layman's terms, and listing the experiments made by eminent scientists, Deepak Chopra has made the quantum world compelling to his readers and listeners. He has challenged them to understand that the nature of reality is simply energy fields, matter fields, electromagnetism, gravity, strong and weak interactions; that these forces come from one unified field of which mind (and our minds are part of reality) is a part; that at a fundamental level, matter, energy and information are identical and that 'to think is literally to create.' Deepak Chopra talks of the 'superstition of materialism', i.e. the belief that the only things that exist are those that our five senses can pickup. This, he says, belongs to the sixteenth century Newtonian model of physics which has been supplanted by evidence from the new twentieth century understanding of physics. The physicist Professor Francisco Varela[11] tells us that we must realise that all things substantial are insubstantial. Commenting on this very fact, psychologist, writer and speaker Wayne Dyer[12] suggests that if we take a microscope and place it on an animate or inanimate object, all we will see are particles. If we turn up the magnification on one particle, all we will see in either case is wave energy. In other words, wave energy underpins everything that looks solid. Deepak Chopra describes this as follows: 'Everything that you see is ultimately made up of atoms; these atoms are made up of particles that are moving at lightning speeds around huge empty spaces and those particles themselves are not material objects but fluctuations of energy in a field of energy.'[13] So, why do we get the realities that we see? The answer is our thinking. Thought, Dr Chopra says, comes from the field of all possibilities (the unified field) but we constrain those possibilities because of the way we 'structure conditioned responses in our life as a result of interpretations of our own memories linked to certain experiences. Then,' he says, 'we get imprisoned in the conceptual framework/boundaries of our interpretations.'[14] So, we imprison ourselves by the ideas of our own imagination. This means that the crucial difference between life and death, success and failure is an interpretation. Hence the explosion of thought management programmes, tapes and CDs in the past ten or so years all exhorting the individual to get into that deep place within themselves and change their 'conceptual boundaries'. However, individual action alone is insufficient to clean out some of the deep-seated subconscious though patterns that lie within us. The collective consciousness of our society is part of the unified field, according to Dr Chopra, and it is affecting our consciousness. So, if we really want change, then we have to 'change that collective mind-set which has become programmed and structured along very rigid conceptual frameworks.'[15] This is one of the many reasons that companies have offered mind-management and personal development programmes not only to their employees, but also to their families and communities.

The impact of collective thinking has been highlighted by the work of physicist Professor Alain Aspect[16] of the University of Paris and Institute Optique, Orsay (France), who showed that all electrons talk to one another in a sort of 'thought internet' and by Biologist, Rupert Sheldrake[17] who identified 'morphic fields' – consistently held thought patterns held by plants, animals, individuals, groups and places that affect the thinking of those who come in contact with the morphic fields. Sheldrake has shown that the morphic field of one group, e.g. animals, can affect the morphic field of another – hundreds of miles away – as the 'data' is passed via that 'electron internet'. Physicist David Bohm, in his book *The Special Theory of Relativity*,[18] documents his discovery that thought is largely a collective phenomenon. He compares collective thought to an 'electron sea' and says that when we think a thought, that thought is immediately registered in a collective sea of thought (the unified field) which can influence individual thinking. So, our thinking about a person, a place etc affects that person, place etc; one person thinking poorly of another person, function, situation, 'thing' can encourage others to do the same; likewise, one person thinking positively of another person, function, situation, 'thing' can encourage others to do the same.

Dr Candace Pert,[19] pharmacologist and psychoneuroimmunologist, discovered neuropeptides – the biochemical equivalent of thought. When we think a thought, the brain releases the biochemical equivalent of that thought. Dr Pert also discovered that there are receptors to the neuropeptides, not just in the brain, but in other cells of the body and that these cells, via their receptors, eavesdrop on the brain to find out what chemical is being released and then release that chemical in the cell. So, each cell of our body is a 'thinking cell' and we are the managers of our internal chemical thermostat. If I think 'I hate my job' then the biochemical equivalent of that thought will be released not just in my brain, but in every cell of my body simultaneously. I will power myself down. If I experience joy, then every cell in my body will simultaneously register the biochemical equivalent of joy. This knowledge puts full responsibility for motivation *entirely* on the shoulders of the individual because, in spite of what the individual is experiencing, s/he can always *choose* how s/he will respond to that experience; s/he can choose how to *interpret* that experience and in doing so, set her/himself free from conditioned responses.

These scientific findings have sparked a huge interest – represented in the number of books and CDs sold – in the ever expanding personal development arena as people try to understand how they can function effectively in a world which has been completely redefined by the quantum model.

(4) General characteristics

- *Use of Eastern philosophies*
  Another major factor in the emergence of spirituality in organisations is that many organisations no longer choose science and technology as the only answer to solve business problems. Instead, more companies are using eastern philosophies such as Confucianism and Zen Buddhism which emphasise group loyalty and finding a spiritual centre in any activity.

- *Use of other philosophies*
  According to writer James Moravec,[20] there are seven aspects of our lives which need to be nurtured in order that we grow into well-balanced, adequate individuals. These are: optimum physical health; rewarding family life and relations with primary others; opportunities for mental stimulation and growth; the ability to express one's emotional experiences; job satisfaction; the ability and the time to have fun; and an ever-deepening and enriching relationship with our Creator. Deepak Chopra[21] lists job satisfaction as the second of the two indicators of life expectancy – personal happiness being the first indicator.

- *Within every culture*
  Every culture has its spirituality – even those that do not subscribe to the Divine. For the Soviets, in the absence of the Divine, education, the arts, sport and accumulating Western objects all became focal points onto which the innate spiritual energy of the people was applied. Each culture reflects its spirituality through its religious traditions, its art, the day-to-day behaviours of its people.

- *Essence of all traditions*
  Spiritual intelligence in the workplace has been experienced

as essence. This is not surprising when we consider the scientific findings corroborating SQ. The fact that there is a God Spot in the brain and that a 40Hz oscillation brings the individual to that deepest place within her/himself, means that there will, of course, be individuals who are connecting with this part of their 'equipment' and experiencing the Divine within everything. It is the individual at this level who can transcend the distractions of the IQ and EQ and see beyond the traditions they represent to the core from which the traditions emerged.

- *The difference between ego and self*
  Different traditions express ego and self differently. Zohar and Marshall[22] provide the very helpful image of the lotus: its petals represent the outer, personality layer of the individual (ego); the middle layer of the petal leaf represents the cultural, tribal layer with its conditioned responses; and the core of the lotus where all the petal leaves meet represents the Divine Centre (self). What all the descriptions of ego and self boil down to is that we have a superficial layer represented by the ego: our personality, our self (lower case self as in self-reliance, self-pity) which is in pursuit of material success. We have a deeper layer represented by the Self: the Spirit within, God-reliance, God-confidence. Spirituality in the workplace includes seeing ego/self as a leech and going through the process of removing the leeches of ego/self in order to release the Self/indwelling Spirit of Truth. The opportunity to do this presents itself each day in how the individual responds to each situation and each person s/he meets.

- *Wholeness*
  The research of Mitroff and Denton[23] highlights that those they studied did not want to compartmentalise or fragment their lives and that these people were on a constant search

for meaning, purpose, wholeness and integration. From the scientific research documented above, this sense of meaning and wholeness can only come when the individual connects with their spiritual centre, i.e. when they experience 40Hz oscillations in the brain. Because their SQ is part of their 'equipment', people cannot leave spirituality at home or just consider it on a Sabbath day, and because people spend so much time now at work, they want to feel free to express it at work too.

- *Presence within*
  Spiritual intelligence at work has also come to mean 'letting one's light shine', being aware of that which comes from within and the inner experience of the individual when s/he comes to experience something 'beyond' her/himself. Spending time at our spiritual centre and, therefore, connecting to the Divine, means that everything we do is pervaded by that Presence. Many great mystics, such as Kahlil Gibran[24], have spoken of the life within while St Catherine of Avila[25] describes the many 'rooms' in the 'interior castle'.

- *Journey within*
  Writing about the 'Turn to the Spiritual in Workplace Training and Development', Professors Tara Fenwick and Elizabeth Lang of the University of Alberta[26] describe a journey into a desert in which there is a discernment of and surrender to an essential nothingness and eventually a spiritual rebirth. Zohar and Marshall[27] suggest that there are six paths on the journey towards greater spiritual intelligence: the paths of duty, nurturing, knowledge, personal transformation, brotherhood and servant leadership. So there is not just one way to be spiritually intelligent. The depth of spiritual intelligence is measured by how close to the Divine Centre was the motivation for an

action or a word. During the journey (which never ends while the individual is on this earth), the process of removing leeches of ego/self is a constant. So, spiritual intelligence is not a final state or a checklist of things to be undertaken. It is a constant process of cleansing oneself of the leeches of ego/self in order to release more of the indwelling Spirit. And the greater the challenge to the ego/self, the greater the release of the indwelling Spirit as the 'space' taken up by the leech of ego/self falls off so that the true Spirit can flow unhindered to the extent of that space.

- *Love*
Love in the workplace, as an expression of spirituality, takes on many forms. For example, for the organisation: having a warm, caring process for welcoming new employees including providing them with a 'buddy' for the first month who will meet the employee for lunch and introduce her/him to others besides 'showing the new employee the ropes'. It includes setting values that ensure that the quality of love is allowed to circulate throughout the organisation so that employees feel valued, important and respected. It is reflected in work systems that support the well-being of the employee. Among other things, Organisational Behaviour Consultant and writer Roger Harrison[28] suggests that love can be expressed in the workplace by 'Looking for the good and the positive in others and acknowledging it when you find it; nurturing the growth of employees: teaching, supporting, encouraging smoothing the path; responding actively to others' needs and concerns; giving help and assistance when it is not your job and treating employees feelings as important.' For the individual, love in the workplace is expressed by genuine compassion for one's colleagues; allowing that love to permeate all of one's activities as an act of love of God and colleague; it is the

'exchange of love, energy, kindness and caring';[29] when it is high in spiritual intelligence, love is transformative, releasing the individual into a higher expression of her/himself and allowing the other person to act beyond her/himself.[30]

- *Peace*
Time to think, peace to listen to what we are thinking and time to process all of that so that we can function within the flow of the unified field is an expression of peace as an aspect of spirituality in the workplace.[31] Staying with the quantum concept, peace is expressed as the 'still, silent 'ocean' on which existence appears as 'waves' [oscillations of energy]... the quantum vacuum... very like what mystics have called the 'immanent God''; the 40Hz neural oscillation experience which connects the individual to this quantum vacuum.[32] In this context it is clear why Socrates warned against 'the barrenness of a busy life'.

- *Space*
Closely associated with peace is space to dream, wonder and create the sense of the spiritual. This has become important for CEOs and managers as part of the spiritual paradigm.[33]

- *Change boundaries, ask fundamental questions*
When the individual is spiritually intelligent, s/he is using that part of their equipment that allows them to question rules and boundaries for their validity and that allows the individual to be creative about how things 'could be'. Spiritual intelligence allows 'what if' scenarios to be played out. This is a vital skill in today's business environment in which the goal posts change often and sometimes from day to day.

 Spiritual Intelligence also allows discussion on moral issues so that rules that are counterproductive to or repressive of the human being, for example, in an organisation, can be revisited so that the rules become more organic, taking into consideration that the organisation is a living entity and therefore must grow with its people needs and customer needs. Emotional intelligence[34] only allows for discussion *within* the existing rule or boundary and so does not have the progressive, transformative nature of spiritual intelligence.

- *Belief in a bigger picture*
  Being able to exit the limitations of one's existing boundary (the organisation) to see that there is more to life (family, hobbies, serving the community), that is, to enter into many other boundaries, is another expression of spiritual intelligence in the workplace. Being able to see the bigger picture brings balance into the individual's life as well as an openness to diversity; it opens up the individual to dream and to conceptualise across a whole range of boundaries so that decision-making is much richer, more encompassing. Today's de-layered organisations require fast, penetratingly concise decisions that work for all aspects of the business. Today's manager is often beleaguered by the pressing problems of the moment so that it is difficult for her/him to engage in this richer thinking. Spiritual intelligence provides the wherewithal for this manager to make quality decisions even when operational problems are pressing. For Robert Greenleaf, leadership mentor and author of many texts on leadership, 'Foresight is a characteristic that enables the servant-leader to understand the lessons from the past, the realities of the present and the likely consequence of a decision of the future. It is deeply rooted within the intuitive mind.'[35] And the intuitive mind resides in our spiritual core.

- *Harnessing spiritual energy in the workplace*
  Mitroff and Denton's research[36] showed that most of the people they studied believed strongly that organisations

must harness the immense spiritual energy within each person in order to produce world-class products and services. However, other analysts of the subject[37] caution that the use of spirituality for profit will not produce the profit desired because it is coming from an inappropriate motivation. This would be in line with the concept of the unified field in quantum theory – that our deep-seated primordial thoughts create realities. So, if my inner motivation is wrong, then I will create the effects of that wrong inner motivation.

- *What executives say*
  The Mitroff and Denton study of corporate America found that executives felt that seeing spirituality as 'soft stuff' was outmoded and irrelevant to the issue, and that this is a subject that must be discussed because it is a key determinant of organisational performance. Although a narrow majority felt that the subject should be discussed outside of the workplace, executives said those who were spiritually developed were more successful and contributed more to the organisation and that spirituality could be measured. Therefore, executives saw spirituality as 'the ultimate competitive advantage'.

- *Growth in prayer groups and spiritual practices at work*
  In the past ten years in corporate US, prayer groups and spiritual practices have emerged at an ever-increasing rate. Corinne McLaughlin[38] notes that 'the American Stock Exchange has a Torah study group, Boeing has Christian, Jewish and Muslim prayer groups; Microsoft has an on-line prayer service; the banking firm, Sutro and Co in California offers "lunch and learn" torah classes, defence manufacturer Northrop Grumman offers Koran classes; Wheat International Communications in Reston, Virginia, has morning prayers open to all employees, but not required.

Spiritual study groups at noon are sometimes called "Higher Power Lunches" – replacing the usual "power lunches". The *Los Angeles Times* recently reported that Marketplace Ministries of Dallas placed freelance chaplains at 132 companies in 38 states. Fellowship of Companies for Christ International, based in Atlanta, has 1500 member companies around the world. They promote "The practise of prayer in company decisions; a commitment to excellence; and 'do unto others in the workplace as you would have them do unto you.'" In addition to prayer and study, other spiritual practices at companies include: "mediation, centring exercises such as deep breathing to reduce stress; visioning exercises; building shared values; active, deep listening, making action and intention congruent and using intuition and inner guidance in decision-making." According to a study at Harvard Business School published in the *Harvard Business Review*, business owners credit 80% of their success to acting on their intuition.'

(5) Personal characteristics

There are fifteen characteristics which emerge as personal or individual expressions of spirituality at work. These are: *Starting with yourself, Taking personal responsibility for one's life, Greater meaning and purpose, Personal satisfaction, Internal motivation, Using gifts and talents to full potential, Search for truth, Beingness, Finding yourself, Being authentic, Way of perceiving reality, Level, Facing fear* and *The role of crisis.*

We will look at these in detail now.

- *Starting with yourself*
  For the individual, spirituality starts with a crisis that leads the individual away from her/his current value system and on to a search to discover 'truth' and meaning. Obviously, this is a very personal search because truth and meaning will resonate differently with the individual at different times

during the search. This happens because the search involves a shedding of ego/self and this causes more and more truth to be revealed, causing meaning to take on different hues and shapes for the individual seeker. Thus, the search or journey process for each individual will be unique because each person will shed those aspects of ego/self that are ready to be shed. Individuals on such a journey have found that, as they have transformed themselves, they have had a wonderful effect on those around them without even knowing it, since more of the 'eternal presence' is flowing through them and less of the divisive and limiting ego/self.

Writer Richard C. Whiteley[39] asks individuals to 'think of a time, be it at work, volunteering, playing on a sports team whatever, when they were totally absorbed, when everything was cooking for them. They generally say things like "I felt incredibly motivated. I felt productive. I had no sense of time. I had fun." That, to me, is beginning to articulate what spirituality, in terms of self-engagement and fulfilment, is all about.'

'Starting with yourself' has come to mean in the workplace that if change is to be achieved it must begin with the individual, because 'corporations don't change – people do.'[40] So, change management programmes must facilitate the ability to change within the individual first, before that individual can even begin to absorb the new changes required by the organisation. It is also important for leaders to understand that they can only facilitate transformation in their Teams to the extent of their own level of transformation. So, if the leader is expecting even better performance, a change agent who is at a level beyond that of the leader, is needed to bring both the leader and the Team to that next level. The higher we go in spiritual development, the more open we need to be to the 'closet' areas of our lives. Some are not willing to go into those secret places and clean them out and so their growth is stunted. Yet, this baggage has to be cleared as Joe Jaworski[41] found: 'A crucial part of our life's journey is the struggle to overcome our accumulated baggage in order to ultimately operate in the flow of the unfolding generative order [what in quantum theory is called the unified field]...our world, our communities, our organisations will change only if we change.'

• *Taking personal responsibility for one's life*
Shifts of mind are not easy to make happen, however. They are borne, it would seem, out of great discipline and difficult choices. Each day brings its situations and people who trigger in the individual a line (or lines!) of old ego/self software. A decision has to be made there and then: do I preserve my old ego/self or create a new self, based on my Divine self? If the individual has the courage to shed the old and create the new, then there will be the inevitable pain of 'surgery', but afterwards, the exhilaration of having the power to make such change. If the individual does not choose the change but prefers to preserve her/his ego/self then the individual experiences more repression, a sense of having lost more ground than they had when the challenge first appeared. It is at this juncture that the individual could take false comfort from food, alcohol, drugs, etc.

This process of transformation requires going upstream, against the great tide of public opinion. It means giving up being 'normal'. With each experience, the individual discovers who they were and sheds that for who they now want to be; they discover what they stood for and what they now want to stand for. This is a time when the individual is both very vulnerable (because s/he is undergoing ego surgery) and powerful (because they are allowing their spirit-centre to govern their heart and mind). It is a time when there will be failures, as the individual finds that some situations are too overwhelming for their courage or discipline, and so they have to meet that challenge again and perhaps again before they are strong enough to win through. As writer Alice Mack[42] puts it, 'Doing one's internal work requires confronting the pain of how parenting and societal programming have damaged the essence of our unique soul... [we have to] go to work for the spiritual component, undergoing what might be considered 'legitimate suffering' on the journey, but the outcome is an expanded consciousness and a renewed capacity for creativity, learning and personal fulfilment.'

This 'massive clean up' is clearly essential if an individual, and particularly a leader, is to effect change and positively impact their workplace. If thoughts create realities, as is the case in the quantum model, then no amount of change management work will have any great impact if the change agents are still creating the wrong realities with their deep-seated thoughts. As Robert Quinn[43] puts it: '*He* is not driving you crazy, you are driving yourself crazy. The issue is not what he is doing; rather, the issue is how you are reacting to him.'

- *Greater meaning and purpose*
  Longer working hours and the consequent diminished time for family, friends, community and religious worship have caused employees to search for the meaning to their lives. Cut off from the spiritual centre they either know or don't know exists, employees are bereft of the brain experience, the 40Hz neural oscillations, that could put their lives in context and provide creative ways of dealing with their situations. So, they struggle with their IQ and EQ, working *within* the boundaries of their situations, not able to see beyond those boundaries (because as discussed earlier, neither IQ nor EQ can go beyond boundaries). They feel trapped, helpless. No wonder Tanis Helliwell[44] said 'Our souls are starving. Everywhere I go, I sense a chronic low grade depression in people, a soul sickness... These are all

symptoms of unhappiness that people feel when their lives and work are not in keeping with their soul's purpose.'

The need to break free from the hold that EQ and in particular IQ have had on the analysis of work is underscored by Fr Matthew Fox's[45] comment that 'the job crisis is something deeper; a crisis in our relationship to work and the challenge put to our species to reinvent it... work comes from the inside out; work is the expression of our soul, our inner being.' So without the use of SQ – spiritual intelligence – in which lies the ability to reframe any situation, it is impossible to reinvent work, and our organisations – out of kilter with the needs of their people – become dysfunctional, ineffective and stressful.

The issue of 'vocation' is raised in the discussion around greater meaning and purpose at work. Writer Gregg Levoy[46] has written about the need for people to return to the idea of having a vocation – something they want to do or even be – instead of being drawn into a job that does not relate to their 'life purpose'.

Up until the mid-1970s in the US and until the late 1980s in Ireland, security of employment was the main source of meaning for employees. In a downturn in the global economy, we might see security return as a prime meaning provider for employees. However, since those years, employees have been looking for more than just a pay-cheque from their workplace. They have expressed needs of a deeper nature. So why have organisations not placed a priority on the issue of meaning? Richard Barrett[47] suggests that 'the majority of our organisations operate from the lower levels of consciousness. They are stuck in the values of survival, relationship or self-esteem consciousness. The only way forward is transformation.' Robert Quinn[48] suggests that the answer to the question lies in part in the fact that the 'normalised work tends to destroy purpose and rewards compromise, transaction and exchange.'

What gives employees meaning? The Mitroff and Denton study[49] showed that the ability to realise full potential as a person was the number one factor; the second was being associated with a good/ethical company; the third factor was having interesting work and the fourth was making money. The joint fifth factor was having good work colleagues and being of service to humankind, while the sixth factor was service to future generations. The seventh was service to their immediate community.

In any search for meaning, it is understandable that the individual would go through various stages before arriving at the spiritual. Using Zohar and Marshall's image of the lotus flower, the search for meaning may begin at the superficial layer of the ego (personality), then the individual may try the distractions associated with the middle layer (culture, tradition, group activities, norms) before finally experiencing true meaning at the centre of the lotus – their Divine Centre. Our Western media pays so much attention to the superficial layer of the ego that it can be difficult for those on a journey not to get sidetracked: there are consumer items to meet the needs of all personality types – cooking utensils, fashion, objets d'art, home decorating, cars, boats, music, books. All of these can easily distract the individual into thinking that they are meeting a deep need within themselves. But this 'deep need' is merely at the superficial 'ego/self' level. In the West, group activities (a middle layer activity), such as sports matches, theatre, concerts/gigs, provide many people with a pseudo-euphoria they could mistake for the spiritual. Once again, the true seeker discovers that the answer does not lie in these arenas. Peter Vaill[50] describes this process in this way: 'Spirituality seeks fundamentally to get beyond materialist conceptions of meaning... [it is] a decision to search beyond what one can do to and/or within oneself. It perceives the inadequacy to fundamentally lie not in the external props, but in the self that would do the propping! Thus, to be spiritual is to try to turn away from all the props entirely and to open oneself to a transcendent source of meaning.'

- *Personal satisfaction*

For many people,[51] spirituality is achieving a sense of personal satisfaction. However, in order to pull away from the external props that drag the individual back to the superficial layers of the ego and culture, what is needed is some deep probing as to why we want what we want. Will getting what we want really give us what we are looking for? In his book *Manifest your Destiny,*[52] Wayne Dyer tackles this issue by asking his readers to consider the feelings that they would experience were they to get the thing they want, i.e. more money (feelings of security, perhaps?), nice figure (feelings of approval?), nice car (feelings of acceptance?) and so on. So some deep questioning is required to stop the pull of external props in order to get at those deep needs that lie behind the desire.

From a purely statistical point of view, the Study of Business Performance by the Wilson Learning Corporation[53] found that 39% of the variability in corporate performance is attributable to the personal satisfaction of the staff and an article from the group Work's Alive identifies four factors associated with personal satisfaction: the relationship with co-workers, work itself, leadership and work performance. The same article reports on the Cone/Roper Cause-Related Marketing Trends Report of 1999, citing that three out of four consumers polled said they were likely to switch to brands associated with a good cause if price and quality were equal: 'Just like the consumer buying a product, when we identify ourselves with a goal we believe in, then we "buy in" and throw our support into our work... When the spirit is blocked, it results in low morale, low productivity and high employee absenteeism and turnover.'[54]

- *Internal motivation*
  Research shows that spirituality in the workplace is inspired by internal motivation – individuals up and down the chain of command committing to quality work that honours what is in their hearts; to deep personal inquiry; to assessing and reassessing alignment of values and corporate vision; to listening to the ideas of others; to seeing the sacred in diverse belief systems and the opportunities for collaborative relationships that deliver a sum that is more than its parts.

- *Using gifts and talents to full potential*
  Another feature of spirituality in the workplace is that it gives employees the opportunity to use their gifts and talents to the full as they engage in their job responsibilities. We must be careful, however, not to see the output of those gifts and talents – wealth and status – as our life purpose, because if we do, then we have moved from our creative Divine Centre back to the superficial ego/self layer, and whatever creativity and talent we are using will only be functioning at a basic level.

- *Search for truth*
  Because spirituality is a journey involving the shedding of the ego/self layer and culture/tradition layer, the individual is in a constant process of seeing a bit more clearly, but not crystal clearly. This level of clarity only comes when a significant amount of ego and culture layers have been removed and there is a subsequent commensurate release of the Divine Centre (which sees all things clearly). So, to ask the question, 'What is spirituality?' begs the reply, 'What is it for you and for your workplace at this stage of your/its development?' And obviously to the question, 'Will my organisation be more effective and profitable as a result of building up spiritual intelligence in our employees?' the

reply must be, 'Of course – there is research to prove the bottom-line benefits *(see Chapter One);* furthermore, employees become more astute, productive, happy and deeply content. However, the question will change its meaning as spiritual intelligence becomes more the order of the day in your organisation.'

So looking for one-answer-fits-all in the search for truth will bring the seeker up a cul-de-sac. This search for Truth is not about spirituality as the *answer* but about spirituality as the *question* because the search must start with the individual and with where the individual is at. This makes the search tremendously useful for the seeker because it is answering questions of direct and immediate relevance to her/him. One definition for the search for truth that has emerged in industry and reflects the individual search is: 'a process by which one discovers inner wisdom and vitality that give meaning and purpose to all life events.'[55]

• *Beingness*
  It was the 6th century BC Chinese Philosopher, Lao Tzu, who said 'The Way to Do is to Be'. Once values have been established by an individual and by an organisation, the only way those values become real is by living them. Colleagues should be able to tell my values from my behaviours. Employees should be able to tell the organisation's values from the behaviours of its leaders and from its systems and structures. Once we have to resort to telling colleagues what our values are, or displaying on a board what the organisation's values are so that employees 'know' them, we have lost the meaning and purpose of values. We shall look in the next section at values, but suffice to say that the key value for an organisation, if it is to be productive, is trust. And trust only comes if there is integrity, and integrity is the result of walking the talk: when behaviours are aligned with espoused values.

To achieve quality of beingness, the individual *commits* – not to any one or any thing necessarily, but to the process of constantly choosing to shed ego/self in order to release the Divine Centre response for a situation or a person. This is the *act of being creative in the moment*. This is the golden gift given to us each day of releasing Greatness within us as we choose to let go the banal and tawdry response in favour of the Divine response. In a very ordinary moment, we release the extraordinary Presence Within. In the words of the book *God Calling*, 'Great deed or small – what matters is whether it was actuated by My Spirit.'[56]

By being committed to creating her/his response in the moment, the individual can move out of a state of beingness that is self-manipulative in which the inner self-talk says 'If I don't work harder it won't get done'; and out of another state of beingness that is full of guilt in which the inner self-talk says 'I'm not good enough'. The individual can know that as s/he chooses to shed the ego/self response, s/he will be helped in that moment. So the person realises that no matter what befalls them, or how difficult the person is that faces them, they can choose to shed their natural ego/self response in the situation and ask for the release of the Divine Response. This approach is enormously liberating and empowering: liberating because the individual is no longer at the mercy of her/his personality limitations; empowering because s/he knows s/he is connecting to a huge resource that has greater knowledge of the situation/person than they s/he has – a resource that can provide the perfect response in each situation, with each person. This is why those on this path can 'Be still and know that I am God'.[57] As Joe Jaworski discovered, 'We only make the mistakes that we have to make to learn what we're here to learn right now... Instead of controlling life, I ultimately learned what it meant to allow life to flow through me.'[58]

James Moravec describes six characteristics of beingness:[59]

1. very perceptive, sensitive to the person's inner thoughts and feelings;
2. conscious of the individual's level of spiritual and intellectual development, always making sure to address them at the appropriate level;
3. always interested in what the other person is doing while seldom offering unsolicited advice;
4. cautious in not directly pointing out another's flaws but would rather, through a series of questions, lead them to recognise those flaws themselves;
5. never drawn into conflicts that could be better dealt with when directed to the appropriate channel;
6. always able to provide words of comfort: looks for the good and praises it; leaves people with some suggestion that is practical and immediately helpful; always includes in his/her discussion some message of the love of God and the truth that we are loved children of the Most High.

- *Finding yourself*
  As can be seen from our discussion so far, we can find ourselves at one of three levels: the superficial ego/self level represented by the personality; the deeper cultural/tribal/tradition level; and the level of the Divine Centre. Zohar and Marshall lament 'ignorance of the centre, a failure even to know that we have a centre, is the principal cause of spiritual dumbness.'[60]

  Leaders, if they are to effectively lead, must find out who they are spiritually, what they are doing and the contributions they are making. However, as Peter Vaill, too, laments, leaders '...could contemplate tenures of thirty, forty and even fifty years' of accumulating wisdom and leadership skill in pursuing the basic purposes of the organisation, *using essentially the qualities of mind, body and spirit that they had acquired by their late twenties* [my italics]. I call this... the statesman myth.'[61]

- *Being authentic*

  Western society conditions its people to create a persona of who 'the world' – parents, teachers, family, relations, friends – wants us to be: 'We will build layers around us to protect the vulnerability of our true identity so that we will not be "made wrong" for showing that *who we are* is different from *who you are*.'[62] Of course, when we clear the ego and culture layer of our being, then the hooks of society have nothing to catch on to. We become free – free to be ourselves, free to allow the other person to be themselves. We have more energy because we are not pandering to the dictates and demands of the ego/self or culture. Other people pick up that we are 'uncluttered': they sense a free-flowing, uninterrupted 'energy' from us. All of this is positively magnetic because it is so unusual to experience, what Trungpa called, 'authentic presence'.[63]

  However, being authentic can be very challenging in an environment in which executives in particular believe they have to have a 'front'. The authentic person has no 'buttons to be pressed', and so the usual politics with their rewards and punishments, viz. conformity, have no power over this person: they function from a different set of rules and those rules are unknown to the 'front' bearers. Instead of asking 'What does the group expect?', the authentic person asks 'What needs to be done?' This brings enormous honesty into the conversation. Of course, we cannot drop a front until we are strong enough inside for it to be shed. So if we sense that those around us are wearing 'psychological masks' it is a sign that they are spiritually weak, that they haven't as yet begun the process of shedding the ego/self (the author of the front or mask).

  The authentic person is able to catalyse in others a desire

to start the journey towards authenticity, as Zohar and Marshall point out: '...the more that I can be genuine in the relationship, the more helpful it will be. It is only by providing the genuine reality which is in me that the other person can successfully seek for the reality in him.'[64] This view is made on the basis of each person being part of the unified field and that because we are part of that creative field, our thoughts are very powerful. As I have already mentioned, the physicist David Bohm tells us that our thoughts about someone have the power to make that person what we expect of them, without us realising that we are doing this. So, if we are disingenuous, because we presume that to be 'the name of the game', then we are creating that mentality in others. However, sometimes we are completely unaware that we are being disingenuous. Chris Argyris claims that every person has their espoused theory (how they claim to behave) and a theory in practice (how they actually behave).[65] In other words, people engage in hypocrisy and don't see it. In fact, they may actually deny it! If the individual is not prepared to consider the existence of hypocrisy in their life, then this will affect their relationships: they will be creating, according to Bohm, negative factors in these relationships without realising it, but the other parties will certainly pick this up. So, the working community within which that individual operates will not be able to reach its full potential. In fact, it will plateau – especially if the person engaging in the hypocrisy is the leader of the group. This is why Robert Quinn exhorts individuals to close their 'integrity gaps', that is, to examine how they behave against how they claim to behave. However, he warns that this is not a comfortable process because we may uncover unpleasant, negative emotions. It is surgery. Yet, 'when our experience, awareness, feeling and communication are in alignment with one another, we become congruent, that is, we are no longer feeling one thing and saying another or failing to communicate something we should.'[66]

- *Ways of perceiving reality*
  The poet William Blake wrote: 'If the doors of perception were cleansed, everything would appear to us as it is – infinite.' Obviously, if we view life from the perspective of the ego/personality, that picture is going to be very different to the perspective given by the culture/tradition layer, and that picture will be entirely different to the picture given by the Divine Centre. All the first two layers can give us is a set of filters that ultimately divide and separate us from others because they are 'different'.

  In these first two layers is secondary reality – that is, 'reality already interpreted and defined by others before us... unexamined conformity that can limit our perceptions about life and its many possibilities.'[67] This is where the role of 'dialogue' comes in, whereby many people from completely different backgrounds are given the opportunity to share their worldview, without judgement or interruption, in order to allow a 'truth' about life to emerge from the group, like an air bubble rising to the surface. The principle is that the innate intelligence of the unified field will always want to reveal the 'whole' truth about any situation and, therefore, by allowing many varying viewpoints to share their views, the 'whole' picture/truth will emerge. Joe Jaworski notes '...a manager's inner model never mirrors reality – it's always a construct. The scenario process (of dialogue) is aimed at these perceptions inside the mind of a decision maker.'[68] So the person gets the opportunity to re-perceive life leading to deep insights that can help the way they live, their decisions, their journey.

  However, at the Divine Centre, we have no constructs: we connect with the unified field and this perspective takes us from the shackles of a worldview consisting of 'things' and separateness to the freedom of a worldview consisting of relationships, a worldview in which everything that is manifest – whatever we see, touch, feel, taste and hear, whatever seems most real to us – is actually non-substantial. We enter a reality so deep that it is beyond what we can articulate. It is at this place that we realise that meaning is truly in the eye of the beholder (at whatever level they function). We are able to consider the perception of the stakeholders of the organisation from a fresh, truly strategic position, understanding the filters these groups are using to define the organisation and to define themselves.

- *Level*
Obviously, each individual is at a different level: some function from the level of ego, which depends on the reactions and opinions of others, and which, therefore, forces the individual to wear a mask and use their vital energy in coping with the myriad variations of reactions and opinions they might experience. Others function from the level of culture, tradition, tribe, nation, and are controlled by the thinking of their 'group'. However, some have reached their Divine Centre, the highest level (on which there are many successive levels). These people have learned how to become independent thinkers that are untouched by the other levels, that is, they cannot be manipulated by the other levels. How we interpret life, people, events is a reflection of our 'level'. Those at the first two levels cannot, however, understand those at the third, Divine Centre, level. As the mystic Thomas Hamblin[69] puts it: 'We can never explain *with* the intellect things which are *beyond* the intellect… In order to know, we have to *be*. That is to say: if we are to *know* a certain thing, we must *become* the thing we seek to know. For instance, if we would know Love, we must ourselves become Love. Also, we can know God only to the extent that we become Godlike.'

• *Facing fear*

As long as we operate on either of the first two levels of beingness, we will be controlled to some extent by fear. The journey towards the inner core, the Divine Centre, means allowing our structures, our safety nets, our certainties, and our assumptions to be removed, and this invariably triggers in us a fear response. At the first two levels we are reactive (more so at the ego/self level). At the core level we are pro-active; we consciously choose how we will respond and we do this from a place of peace because we know that we are connected to Infinite Intelligence via the unified field. Because we have this peace, our brain functions fully for us; there is no stress and, therefore, no cortisol released to send our brain into a dysfunctional state whereby we easily 'forget'. No, at this Divine Centre of Love we are at peace and all our brain functions work for us and our awareness and intuition work for us to provide the best response in a given situation. This response is a win-win response because Infinite Intelligence, the Divine Centre of Love, always has the interest of the other person at heart as well as our own. Fear responses from the first two layers are usually based on self-interest. Abraham Maslow[70] points out that '...healthy growth is a never-ending series of choices between safety (fear) and growth (love).'

Robert Quinn, speaking of the organisational aspects of fear writes: 'Wherever we find people gathering together as a group, we also find a system of sanctions, that is a network of formal and informal rewards and punishments that are assigned to different behaviour.'[71] The leader functioning from level one (ego) will play safe; to a lesser extent so will the leader functioning from level two (culture). Negative feedback will not be encouraged at level one and gingerly received at level two. The sheer openness of positive confrontation typical of level three (Divine Core) is missing. So, problems prevail and because problems cannot be fully discussed solutions are not forthcoming. The net effect of this is that people feel badly inside, a) because they are allowing this level of behaviour to continue, b) because they are also allowing their Divine Core, their true nature, their potential for greatness, to perish and c) because they are allowing all of this to happen due to their need for approval, to be seen as competent and to be seen as meeting the expectations of their boss. Their insecurities trigger insecurities in others functioning at the same development levels. So, real, productive community becomes impossible as the talents, genius and energy of these people is squandered on reacting to fear.

As we come to the edge of our comfort zone we experience fear. Fear doesn't have to be a negative: it can be the signal to us that we are about to expand into a new dimension,[72] and that to accomplish this we must face yet another fear that existed in us due to the old ego/culture software which is now surfacing to be edited out. Robert Greenleaf recognised the need to face fear and devoted a whole chapter to it in his 1977 text on 'Servant Leadership'.[73]

- *The role of crisis*
  As I write this, just days after the attack on the World Trade Centre in New York and on the Pentagon, I am aware that the ensuing crisis has catapulted many people into a discussion of the real and deeper issues of Life. It is tragic that a crisis is the usual door to spiritual development.[74] Perhaps this is a comment both on how easily distracted we are by our material world (levels one and two of development) and on how embedded we are in Newtonian logic that would deny the existence of anything spiritual and, therefore, place more value on 'more logical' discussions and pastimes. Certainly, Joseph Campbell[75] documents well the call to the hero to regain his soul and, in order to do so, to embark on a journey fraught with

dangers. While it may not be a crisis that propels the hero, s/he soon finds 'ordeals' and 'the supreme ordeal' during the course of the journey that must be faced. And it is in facing these ordeals that the ego structure of the hero is cracked wide open and falls off only to reveal the essence of who s/he has been all along. Fear as a force must be faced and conquered if Love as a force is to be revealed and triumph.

Like individuals, organisations normally have to experience a crisis before the organisation will 'waken up' to a new reality. The only exception to this rule is the 'Values-Based Organisation' which is self-motivated enough to function from its Divine Centre.

(6) The work environment internally supportive of spirituality

Study of this area uncovers many ways in which organisations are working to create a work environment which is internally supportive of spirituality. These are: *understanding that the commonly held view of organisations no longer fits, the general nature of a spiritual workplace, a systems view, the work environment supports the whole person, the importance of vision, personal and work missions are compatible, aligning vision and mission with a higher purpose, the importance of values, making it safe to discuss spirituality, recognising each person as a spirit, creating a place where the soul can soar, fostering connectedness, fostering a sense of community, recognising that each employee has a unique role, appreciation of diversity, communication, listening, the importance of fun, flexibility, seeing spirituality as energy that affects bottom line, releasing creativity, encouraging adhocracy, partnership, leadership facilitating the discovery of spirituality, the importance of role models, being a learning organisation, having inspiriting activities/events/ objects in the workplace, paid time off for community work, having spiritual practices at work, and enhancing the physical environment.*

Let's look at each of these areas in some detail.

- *The commonly-held view of organisations no longer fits*
In the past, organisations were set up to produce goods or provide a service with the purpose of making money. Organisations were their own masters, controlling their own destinies. That has become a very simplistic model. Today, organisations are governed by legislation vis-à-vis the environment, health and safety, gender balance in staffing, discrimination on the basis of colour, creed and sexual orientation. They function in a global economic context that is itself governed by a host of different legislations and political persuasions, yet they must produce the same level of quality and customer service. In order to maintain their relevance to the marketplace, the organisation has become a continuous learning system with departments and their members spread across a host of nations in networks of teams, adhocracies rather than in hierarchies, so that they can be more flexible and responsive to market needs. So, the concept of the organisation as a fixed entity is gone. Today's organisation is fluid, multinational with a lot of international, political and legal savvy.

Talent – intellectual capital – has become the key asset in today's organisation, especially in the seriously downsized organisation in which there is no 'excess' in the system to cope with very busy periods. A company's intellectual capital is what gives it a competitive edge: a team of people who are relaxed, talented, creative, innovative, know how to work together, have eliminated organisational politics in favour of team performance, and feel valued, are going to produce better results than the intellectual capital of an organisation deficient in any of these attributes. So the organisation today is seen as a living entity rather than as the inanimate body it was in the past when systems, procedures and structures were all-important. Boundaries are being removed to facilitate the already stretched company talent in sharing ideas, group creativity and group decision-making and to minimise politics within the organisation.

- *The general nature of a spiritual workplace*
The spiritually intelligent workplace looks after its people; it has outgrown personality struggles, the pettiness of ego/self and the barriers normally erected by entrenched cultural/national or tribal mentalities. It functions from a place that is a common denominator for all peoples: the Divine Centre. So, across all personalities, cultures and gender there is a deep understanding. There is a strong sense of 'we' instead of 'I' because each person knows that they are connected to the other via the unified field. There is a strong sense that each has a window on reality, though not the whole window and that, therefore, there must be non-judgemental sharing of ideas in order to get the complete picture. There is also a strong sense of knowing that the unified field can provide yet another dimension to the sharing of ideas, so in the spiritually intelligent workplace, deep listening takes place in order to catch emerging information. Such a workplace is like a team of rowers all working in synchrony, achieving a synergy, an extra output unachievable via the individual talents of the team.

The spiritually intelligent workplace does not shy from difficult tasks such as firing members when all improvement plans have failed. They are enormously honest environments, confronting issues that would be 'undiscussables' in other organisations and making fundamental changes when needed instead of 'tweaking' the surface for cosmetic purposes. So they carry no baggage and, therefore, the intellectual and emotional energy of their people can be fully focussed on the task at hand.

The Mitroff and Denton Study[76] discovered five different types of spiritually aware organisation: the Religious Organisation, the Recovering Organisation, the Values-

Based Organisation, the Socially Responsible Organisation and the Evolutionary Organisation. The Religious Organisation is that organisation that is governed and taken over by subscription to one particular religion (as opposed to spirituality, but could include spirituality). Recovering Organisations (based on the AA Model) courageously face up to the truth about their failings and are very frank about the extent of hard work needed to create an ethical and spiritually intelligent workplace. The Socially Responsible and Values-Based Organisations focus on leading with values. However, while the Socially Responsible Organisation is comfortable with the term spirituality, discussing spiritual intelligence in the workplace and infusing it into each functional area, the Values-Based Organisation is not. For the Socially Responsible Organisation, the spiritual development of the individual and organisation is a must at this point in history and 'cannot be attained through traditional educational. programmes alone. It also cannot be left to chance. It must be the result of an explicitly designed, systematic and sustained effort... The notion of constantly taking audits, admitting one's errors and making direct amends should be vitally important design features of spiritually-based organisations.'

It would seem that the challenge for the Values-Based Organisation is to evolve beyond itself to embrace its spiritual intelligence. The Mitroff-Denton Study showed that spiritually intelligent organisations have employees who: '1) are less fearful of their organisations 2) are far less likely to compromise their basic beliefs and values in the workplace 3) perceive their organisations as significantly more profitable 4) report that they can bring significantly more of their complete selves to work, specifically their creativity and intelligence and 5) are hungry for models of practising spirituality in the workplace without offending their co-workers or causing acrimony... they are hungry not only to express their souls, but also to further the development of their innermost selves.' The Evolutionary Organisation usually begins with a strong association with a particular religion and evolves to a more ecumenical position. This type of organisation is very comfortable with discussing spiritual intelligence and applying it to enhance the company.

- *A systems view*
  The discovery in quantum physics of the unified field has done a great deal to underscore the need to view all things from a systems perspective. Organisation design expert, writer and speaker Margaret Wheately provides a practical application of this theme to leadership and the organisation citing the fact that the atomic world is a dynamic world in which particles appear and disappear like waves from the deep, still atomic ocean and that the modern organisation can learn from this in having more flexible structures in which employees gather to do a job and then disband. However, this can only happen in a spiritually intelligent organisation that a) provides its people with a strong sense of community beyond their immediate team, so that when a team of people disband there is no loss of identity or meaning and b) trains its leaders how to lead an impermanent team; how to be internally motivated rather than motivated by the size or type of team they manage.[77]

  Peter Vaill looks at the systems view from the angle of how we respond to life and comments that whatever we do, we do out of a complex range of reasons and that 'A whole system of values was at play in our awareness and feeling of ourselves and it was a system in our awareness and not just a list.'[78]

  Systems must be considered when we are effecting change in the organisation. If we change one element, it will have a domino effect on the others. So if we change culture, we must change strategy, structure and systems and vice versa. Tools to effect such systems change are future search, dialogue, leadership development and corporate coaching of individuals.

- *The work environment supports the whole person*
  Consultant Heather Skelton suggests '...creating healthy environments to support the whole person. Both large companies and small entrepreneurial shops are realising that a healthy employee is a more effective employee and that health is not just physical, that much physical illness comes from the environment and from emotional and spiritual deprivation.'[79] She suggests that employees be allowed to decorate their own workspace with fabrics and colours that uplift the spirit and that the company restaurant provide healthy food. Another example of creating a spiritually intelligent physical environment is the use of quiet 'nature spaces' where people can go to reflect, meditate, and the bringing in of light, sun, fresh air. Having energy massage available is also considered part of a healthy environment. An example of such a work environment, comprising all of the above is Nortel Networks' Head Office in Brampton, where there is also a prayer room for different spiritual persuasions. As Heather Skelton says, 'All of this creates your workplace as a community, a place where people come to relate to each other and do meaningful work.'

- *The importance of vision*
  The great Austrian Psychiatrist, Viktor Frankl,[80] documents the time he spent in Auschwitz as a Jewish prisoner in his book *Man's Search for Meaning*. He writes about the importance of keeping that inner picture positive in the face of very grim circumstances. This he did by encouraging himself and a small group of people he helped to picture

themselves doing something significant *that they still had to do*. In other words, he had them focus on a future event. This process gave both him and those he helped a sense of purpose and meaning. He pictured himself standing on the stage of a great auditorium telling people of his time in Auschwitz and what he had learned. This vision propelled him forward.

From the work of Dr Candace Pert[81] we know that the brain reacts chemically to the pictures/thoughts we give it and that the neurotransmitters in our bodies pick up on that chemistry and flood every molecule of the body with it. So, a positive, inspiring picture will release its chemical equivalent in our brain and send the same chemicals right throughout our bodies so that we are truly energised by the picture.

Deepak Chopra reminds us that because we exist as part of the unified field, our lives can express an infinite array of possibilities. We are the ones, who by our limited or even negative thinking, 'freeze' one possibility into our lives. This, Chopra says, is bondage.[82] The unified field is really like a highly creative parent who has a huge box of lego and is prepared to make up whatever their child asks them to make. The outputs are entirely dictated by the scope of the child's thoughts. So, being able to stretch those thoughts beyond the simple dictates of our logic, having a fertile imagination and a positive, determined disposition, all become essential ingredients because of the creative unified field of which we are a part. As the psychologist and writer Wayne Dyer exhorts: 'You'll see it when you *believe* it.'[83]

- *Personal and work missions are compatible*
  Organisation design expert, writer and speaker, Richard Barrett asserts that: 'in the twenty-first century, the most successful organisations will be those that align the personal missions of their employees with the mission of the

organisation.'[84] For many reasons already discussed, it is clear that employees want work that brings meaning to their lives and this they can achieve in part by aligning their own sense of purpose with the purpose of the company. Viktor Frankl makes the point that having something significant still to do is a crucial motivator in vision. We know from work design theory that individuals must see some significance in what they are doing otherwise they will be de-motivated. These factors combined with unprecedented education, training and development of employees in the past forty years have created a workforce of individuals that wants to see how their contribution fits into the whole; how their contribution makes a difference to society. Therefore, an important role for the spiritually intelligent organisation is to help its employees discover their life purpose and to make sure that their work is consistent with that purpose. Martin Rutte quotes a senior vice president: 'Imagine what would happen if you had a company in which all the people were doing their life's work. You would have more loyalty, more resilience, more creativity, more innovation and a deeper sense of self-reliance, self-renewal and self-generation.'[85] The Fast Company have found that: 'People and companies do well, financially and otherwise, to the degree that their interests match their values. To create that alignment, you have to see it. And to see it, you have to find a way to measure it.'[86]

- *Aligning vision and mission with a higher purpose*
  Many companies have found that a launching pad for bringing spiritual intelligence into the workplace is to clarify the company's vision and mission and to align it with a higher purpose and deeper commitment to service to both customers and community.[87]

- *Values*

  Values bond people together like a gluing agent – this is especially so in a multicultural/multinational organisation in which employees from various countries are part of a team or when employees do not apparently value the deeper aspects of life (i.e. when they have not discovered their spiritual intelligence). Values are always there in an organisation. However, if they are not shared, then the values of the strongest character in the 'group' will prevail and this might mean the culture of the organisation dropping to the lowest value set.

  Values shape behaviour, informing employees as to what is acceptable and unacceptable practice in the organisation, and informing clients about how business will be done for them and what kinds of behaviours they can expect to experience during their transaction with the company.

  Shared values create a sense of community because shared values build trust.[88] Lack of shared values destroys trust and breeds anarchy. When this happens, employees become increasingly reliant on rules, contracts and the law, while fear and a sense of separation from others increase. Shared values means that the values are not just espoused but lived and applied in the transactions of the organisation. When the company is hiring or promoting staff therefore, it is important for employees to see that these people walk the company values. Decisions must be made with the company values in mind. The organisation's leaders particularly must practise the company values.

  Values that are helpful to, and have been used to set up, a spiritually intelligent organisation are: cooperation, integrity, acceptance of others, diversity, honesty, good quality, accountability, service, intuition, trustworthiness, respect, justice, fairness, building and maintaining good relationships, keeping one's word, being there for one's family and for others, being in harmony and in touch with the universe, courtesy, modesty, compassion for others, never doing anything you wouldn't want to do to your own family, seeing future generations as fundamental stakeholders, development as opposed to growth, affirming the health and dignity of employees and clients, wholeness of the individual, interconnectedness, hope, love, optimism, sharing, and serving society as a whole. Leadership and management consultant, writer and speaker Fred Harmon places an emphasis on psychological values because he has found that when there is no crisis, leaders 'need clear psychological values to inspire others to action.'[89] And one of those values, according to Harmon, is respecting diversity. The consulting group 'It's Time' declare that 'Spirituality is Respect: respect of self and of others; respect for the environment; other people's personal privacy, their physical space and belongings; different viewpoints, philosophies, religion, gender, lifestyle, ethnic origin, physical ability, beliefs and personality... Rather than criticising the other for being different, we can learn how different people see the world.'[90]

Values attract customers. When values are publicised and connected to something of societal benefit, then customers feel that they are not just buying a product but a whole value system. The organisation obtains 'not just loyalty but a deeper spiritual connection based on shared social values... It offers people a way to connect with kindred spirits, to express their most deeply held values when they spend their money. Unlike most commercial transactions, buying a product from a company you believe in transcends the purchase. It touches your soul.'[91]

Values, however, are not a panacea for well-being and employee motivation in the spiritually intelligent organisation. As Mitroff and Denton demonstrate in this very telling comment: 'Values are not enough. It has to be something more universal. Most of corporate America doesn't realise it, but we are running out of gimmicks to motivate the workforce. The only thing that will really motivate people is that which gives them deep meaning and purpose in their jobs and in their lives in general.'[92]

- *Making it safe to discuss spirituality*
  In many businesses today, spirituality is not discussed because there is more of a focus on 'the business' than on the people. Some organisations are still getting to grips with personality difference, still trying to improve communication and get 'teams' working. However, since spirituality is at the core of the person – whether the individual realises it or not – and the core is what drives motivation, and since more and more people are becoming spiritually active (as can be seen by the number of books being sold in bookstores), it is vital that individuals and groups are encouraged to explore what spirituality means for them. Such a process means acknowledging that there will not be 'just one answer' and being willing to understand another's position.

- *Recognise each person as a spirit*
  In Taylor's *Scientific Management Theory*, people are 'bodies' – brawn and no brain. In McGregor's *Management Theory*, people are people with inner, psychological motivations. Quantum theory and brain research on spirituality show that each person is a spirit and, therefore, this knowledge must be factored in to management and leadership training if the whole person is to be properly led. Abraham Maslow charted the movement between each of these three levels in his *Hierarchy of Needs*. However, in his time, the pinnacle of the hierarchy – self actualisation – related more to emotional and intellectual as opposed to spiritual actualisation. This means that career planning and employee development must include the apex of self actualisation –

spirituality – if the employee is to be truly fulfilled and give the organisation his/her full potential.

- *Work: a place where the soul can soar*
Looking after the financials and developing good systems appease our IQ and are the least complex factors to consider in an organisation. Looking after people appeases our EQ (emotional intelligence). In fact, the new millennium is witnessing many organisations embrace teamwork and community, ethical and caring behaviour, employee involvement in decision-making and the enhancement of the personal growth of employees. The net effect of these behaviours can be seen in productivity, efficiency, quality (the factors directly affecting the financials) and interpersonal relationships. As employees are encouraged to grow personally, they eventually come upon their spiritual nature. Values – and more importantly, living them – nourish the spiritual nature and also the emotional nature, and because our spiritual base, our disposition, accounts for at least 60% of what we communicate[93] then the quality of each interaction with another is high. I may have strong interpersonal skills, but if my disposition is 'spiritually dumb', 60% of my interaction with others will be impaired. The links between the people factor and bottom line have already been made earlier in this book. Something that can enhance the people factor by 60% must be worth looking at.

Many of the conferences on spirituality in the workplace[94] have shown that enlightened organisations are creating a spiritual sanctuary for employees through shared values, love, trust and respect; through apparently opposite values such as discipline and spontaneity, rules and freedom, high expectation and unstinting love; resulting in a place where they can contribute to the aliveness of their colleagues, customers and clients. This has meant having leaders who not only engage the mind with their logic and engage the heart with their passion but leaders who are engaging the spirit with their compassion and beingness. Some organisations setting up have chosen to start by recruiting such leaders and then developing the structure of the business. In the Virgin empire, attitude supersedes experience as a key competence.[95] The company reasons that it can always give people experience, but it is far more difficult to clean out a bad attitude and the effects that can have on other employees. In fact, values compatibility is more important to the spiritually intelligent organisation than hiring or promoting excellent technical people who cannot build trust, respect community and work well with others. Attitude has to do with disposition/spirit. Enlightened organisations are realising that this disposition/spirit factor can make or break productivity and are, therefore, spending time to develop this factor in their employees. Seeing work as a vocation and helping employees get into work that reflects their sense of vocation is another way that enlightened organisations are enabling the soul and motivation to soar. When we work at what we believe our 'mission'/vocation to be, we become highly motivated and proactive – we do not feel that we are working. As the saying goes 'Find a job you enjoy doing and you will never have to work a day in your life'. Community has become an important value and to this end, self-interest has been replaced by the values of collective interest and helping others to achieve their individual interests.

- *Connectedness*
  The human spirit, rooted as it is in the unified field, senses that there is a holy centre of life in which all things are interconnected. And, of course, this interconnectedness is precisely what quantum physics has proven. Those who are spiritual intelligent sense interconnectedness in different forms: an emotional connection to God; connected

relationships; the interconnection of philosophy, business and the environment; recognition and acceptance of individual responsibility for the common good, including humanity and the planet; seeing interrelationships rather than things; making employees feel fully connected to one another, the company, the community to customers and to nature; being connected with one's complete self, others and the entire universe; synchronicity – a meaningful coincidence of two or more events, where something other than the probability of chance is involved;[96] the opportunity to bring wholeness back into situations or people with whom we come in contact.

- *Sense of community*
  Being connected to others meets a fundamental need in human beings for recognition, and many studies[97] have proven that workers are happier in group-oriented organisations than in more individualistic ones. Community means a variety of norms, rules, moral obligations and habits that bind the group together. It provides a 'family feeling'. So, creating a sense of community in the workplace is a vital factor in the well-being and consequent productivity of employees. The modern organisation often pitches employees against one another using apparently objective feedback mechanisms (e.g. 360 degree feedback in which peers, superiors and those they lead are all asked to give their feedback on an employee. However, unless people are made aware of the psychological baggage they carry, and the subsequent filters they have, such feedback mechanisms are far from objective. When they are tied into wages increases/bonus/shares, then the real divisiveness of such feedback becomes clear: what peer is going to give honest feedback if it means that his/her colleague will receive a better bonus or more shares? So, the modern organisation has become a lonely place where for many, they are not

understood but judged, and competition, not cooperation (the true meaning of the Latin root *competere*), is the order of the day, even though substantial evidence exists to prove that 'competition substantially reduces the quality of work or learning that people are engaged in as well as undermining relationship and psychological health.'[98] Compounding this is the long working day that has become the norm for so many employees, who have, as a result, become disconnected from their local, social and even family communities. Our organisation structures, with their vertical, horizontal and external boundaries, have created a sense of separation in employees via status (vertical), self-interest (horizontal) and manipulation and politics (external/geographic). When community collapses, according to Francis Fukuyama, 'individuals cling to their ascriptive identities (family, ethnic group, delinquent communities) all the more fiercely and these provide an easy form of community with which they can avoid feeling atomised, weak and victimised.'[99] Spiritually intelligent leaders, therefore, build strong communities at work by removing fear from the workplace systems and from individuals; by building deeply caring values which are built into the performance management system; by enabling each employee to see that s/he has a unique role to play (e.g. encouraging the employee to consider what gives him/her an inner sense of meaning and immense satisfaction) and helping them to allow other employees to play their own unique role in an attitude of acceptance and non-judgement (so that each employee can experience how liberating and self-motivating it is to live out their true purpose); by supporting the emotional well-being and growth of their employees; by creating rules and discipline that help employees 'avoid excessive waste of psychic energy in the negotiation of what can or cannot be done... then the psychic energy released from bickering and arguing can be invested in the pursuit of each employee's goals';[100] by helping employees to relate to others not from a position of self-interest but from a position of the good of the whole.

- *Appreciation of diversity*
  In a global economy, where colleagues come from different parts of the world, being able to appreciate and enjoy diversity is vital if true teamwork is to emerge. I have already mentioned the negative aspect of boundaries (vertical, horizontal and external/geographic) but psychological boundaries exist and these can prevent the appreciation of diversity. Such boundaries are power, status, gender, race and profession. In the spiritually enlightened organisation, however, such boundaries are removed and even fade away as employees discover their true spiritual core and the unified field that binds them together. They realise that, at their core, they are designed in the same way and that they are each different 'waves' on the quantum ocean.

- *Communication*
  When we consider the number of self-development and assertiveness texts that exist, as well as books on how to survive a dysfunctional family, we realise that many people have been exposed to poor communication processes in their family lives. Large numbers of children in a classroom have forced teachers to opt for minimising the diversity as well as the communication among children so that the lesson can be taught. Communication in these examples is often about staying out of trouble, keeping things on an even keel, keeping a low profile. These kinds of communication pattern do not serve us well in a work environment that requires teamwork and working with diversity. Spiritually intelligent organisations recognise this and look to help their employees shed their old communications programming in favour of one that is

helpful not only to themselves but to the well-being of the whole organisation.

- *Listening*
  Of the four key needs of people (being understood, being respected, being made to feel welcome and having physical and psychological security), being understood is top. Many conflicts happen unnecessarily because someone hasn't taken the time to understand – not agree with, but understand – another. To understand we need to listen, and to listen we need to be fully present with the other person, aware of the nuances in their voice, their body language, what they are and are not saying, reading between the lines, not even trying to put our own point of view forward, but focussing on their view. We need to listen to our own inner voice, take time out to reflect on what we have heard so that the intelligence within what quantum physicists call the 'unified field', in which we all live, can interpret for us what we have heard. Artists and innovators talk of an incubation period (a period of intense contemplation/listening) after they have exposed themselves to the data needed for their 'project'. During the incubation period there is often a 'Eureka!' experience in which new, previously unthought-of ideas are dropped into the mind of the individual. There is so much involved in this type of listening, no wonder it is called 'active listening'! The net effect of this type of listening is that the speaker feels the listener cares about them, their ideas and their thoughts, and this helps the person feel accepted and recognised for their special and unique self.

- *The importance of fun*
  Dr Candace Pert has made it quite clear that for every thought we think, our brain releases the brain chemical equivalent.[101] So we are in charge of our inner climate. We

can change how we feel about life simply by changing how we see the world, how we respond to the world. Fun and laughter release very powerful brain chemistry which makes us feel great. This reduces stress and helps minimise non-clinical depression. So, the many hundreds of thousands of man hours lost each year due to stress and depression can be spared. Spiritually developed organisations understand this and foster fun as a key component in every day work-life. Interestingly, fun triggers the right side of the brain where solution-focussed, creative thinking reside. This is also the side of the brain that allows the individual to juggle many things at the one time, be innovative and creative and, when it sorts out a problem it sorts out the whole problem, not just part of it, as does the left, the serious side of the brain. It is also the side of the brain that is good at forecasting, remaining calm in difficult situations and using intuition – one of the links to our spiritual core. So fun in the workplace brings about these very valuable outcomes!

- *Flexibility*

  We live in a rapidly changing and fragile world – economically, socially and politically. Companies downsize and suddenly part of the workforce has to go and find work again: new job, new environment, and perhaps new house. Today's person must be flexible and open to change. This is in line with our understanding of modern physics and the nature of the unified field, which offers an infinite array of possibilities and waits for our deep-seated thoughts to choose one of those. The spiritually dumb person gets locked into one mode of reality, not realising the great gift of our innate design: that our thoughts direct and shape our lives. So, change management becomes a slow process – too slow for the fast pace of today's competitive environment. Effective organisations know this and offer programmes to help their employees 'get out of their thought ruts'.

- *Seeing spirituality as energy that affects bottom line*
  The 60% which we communicate – our disposition – is often experienced by people as 'energy'. We have often said that the atmosphere of a match was electric or that you could cut the atmosphere in a meeting with a knife! These are phrases in our vernacular attempting to express this energy that we are. When we become aware that we 'carry' an energy (that we are an energy) then we can ask ourselves: is that energy positive or negative? Positive thoughts and feelings will always create a positive energy, and negative thoughts and feelings will always create a negative energy. Spiritually developed organisations check the quality of the individual and collective energy in their organisations regularly. Negative energy is released, for example, when there is violence, harassment, discrimination, verbal abuse, lack of respect, or loss of productivity. Positive energy is released when employees feel respect from their management and colleagues, when they are free to express their opinions, when they are given control over the shape of their work environment through shared decision making with the management team, and when they are nurtured and refreshed by social and other activities and communities outside of work.

- *Releasing creativity*
  In an economic environment in which similar products are offered at similar prices, service has become a defining competitive edge. When companies offer the same level of service, then innovation and creativity become a matter of economic survival. Studies of children ages three to five[102] reveal that 98% of the children scored in the genius category. Between the ages of eight to ten only 32% scored in that category. Between ages thirteen to fifteen only 10%. Two hundred thousand adults over the age of twenty-five have taken the same tests and only 2% scored at the genius level.

The human being is uniquely creative of all the species – made, according to the world's great religions, in the image and likeness of God. So, at the core of the human is the desire to create. Enlightened organisations understand this and look for the many ways in which creativity is stifled in their organisations – not just to re-motivate their employees, but to tap that creative pulse that is critical to the survival of the company. Enlightened organisations build creativity into their performance management systems so that they are rewarding the creative, the forward thinking, perhaps even the outrageous! Such organisations provide training and development in this area and many have offered music, painting, dancing, poetry, colour therapy or cooking to stimulate the creative centre of their employees as well as programmes which encourage employees to see things differently, to break out of habits, outdated beliefs and find new ways of thinking, doing and being.

- *Encouraging adhocracy*
  There have always been informal networks of self-managed teams in organisations, it is just that now, with regular downsizing, employees are having to regroup more regularly to consider how to get the job done effectively with less people, and perhaps with a boss whose base is on the other side of the globe. In this type of scenario, leadership and management take on a very different complexion. In some cases, the employees have to be self-managing and self-led. This requires great inner resources of the employee and an understanding of how exactly to go about the process! There are other scenarios in which the organisation, like a huge liner, is set on a course – and to deviate from that course to explore an interesting activity on the horizon would take much longer than if a small boat were sent out to survey the scene. This small boat is the adhocracy, created when there is a need to explore a new

opportunity and when fast reaction is required. So, adhocracies arise out of change and we live and work in a world of constant change. The spiritually intelligent organisation fosters adhocracy as a necessary complement to flexibility and creativity so that the organisation remains relevant not just to its marketplace but also to its employees.

* *Partnership*
  The rationale for adhocracy underscores the importance of partnership. In a de-layered or downsized organisation, sometimes a product or a line or a job is still running (i.e. it has not been shelved) and those who are left are doing the work of those who are gone. In this context, partnership is critical: I must take individual responsibility for my area and trust that other people will perform according to their responsibilities and commitments for the good of the team, and not just for the good of themselves. In a highly democratic society, employees look for partnership: they want psychological ownership and this they can get in the organisation that provides shared decision-making, open-book management, and stock ownership. Rosabeth Moss Kanter[103] highlights that in a world charged with change, employees look to 'steady the boat' through some sense of control in aspects of their lives. If the workplace can give the employee that sense of control, then that feeling of being in control mitigates the effects of change in other arenas of life. Partnership involves moving away from *telling* someone that something should be done or using forms of leverage such as threat of being fired, i.e. *forcing*. Instead, partnership involves open dialogue and pursuing win-win strategies to achieve results.

* *Leadership facilitates the discovery of spirituality*
  In The Living Company, Arie de Geus states that 'companies die because their managers focus on the economic activity of producing goods and services and they forget that their

organisation's true nature is that of a community of humans.'[104] Not only is the organisation a community of humans, today's organisation is a community of informed, educated, democratic and oftentimes intellectually, emotionally and spiritually intelligent humans. Such people look to be led by someone better than they are; by someone who has gone further in the personal development than they have; by someone who is walking the talk; by someone who has the capacity to empower them *at their level*. They want a leader with whom they resonate, who has vision, and who has the courage to pursue that vision and maintain it in difficult circumstances. They want a leader who speaks and acts for them, who echoes what is in their heart – expressed and unexpressed. Not only that, today's employee is looking for an environment reflective of his/her values or of values that s/he can admire and be inspired by. The creation of such an environment is the responsibility of the leader.

In the past, common characteristics of leaders were that: they focus on vision, values and motivation; they see the big picture and the interconnections (they are strategic); they think long term; through their personal disposition they reach and influence people well outwith the scope of their normal function; they are aware of the fact that politics exist and have mastered the most effective way of dealing with both positive and negative politics; they constantly renew themselves and their organisations: constant renewal is important to them; they inspire, intellectually and emotionally, captivating the minds and hearts of their people. However, today, in a world of disintegrating organisational, institutional and social structures, the employee wants more. S/he is looking for someone who can penetrate right to his/her core; a leader who can inspire at the deepest of levels and provide meaning and hope in difficult times. This really means that the leader has to go beyond merely reflecting good values.

The leader of today is expected to have enormous courage and guts – and that comes only from having gone through the ordeals described by author Joseph Campbell[105] and having learned from those ordeals. These are the 'fiery furnaces' that burn the dross of fear, ego and cultural dictates off the 'hero' only to leave the gleaming gold of core spirit – the spirit of love and compassion. In this way, the leader required for these times has thrown off all the baggage that would prevent him/her from relating to everyone – to all personalities, all races, each gender so that s/he cuts right to the quick, right to the soul of those s/he leads. But the pain and loss experienced in such 'fiery furnaces' cause many to shy away so that their 'leadership span' can only stretch to those personalities, races, gender with which they are comfortable. The best they can do is reflect good values and create the environment in which those values thrive. But there is something about the disposition of this leader that is unresolved and 'the led' pick that up. It is the leader who has gone through many ordeals and a supreme ordeal, who has cleared their disposition so that their core, their spirit, has room to expand its vastness through their presence – it is this person who connects to the deep places within 'the led'. Such a person will be humble, but they will have a big presence. It is this person who can facilitate transformation in others: we cannot give what we haven't got. Since this type of leader has cleared the path as it were, to reach right into the centre of his/her being, so s/he is able to coach others to do the same – to move beyond how they perceive a situation (their IQ), and past how they feel about a situation (their EQ), into what they might do about a situation and their motives for doing that (SQ). When we reach the core of ourselves, we have reached love and 'love that is high in spiritual intelligence, (i.e. unconditional love) is transformative – it releases us into a higher expression of ourselves and allows the other to reach beyond himself.'[106]

Strengthened by the fact that quantum physics is focussing attention on the inner as opposed to the outer facts, strategies, goals and appearances which the Newtonian world emphasises, the spiritually-intelligent leader can provide a model and rationale for constructive introspection and thought management so that the journey towards discovery, esteem and celebration of spirit can take place. Employees can be taught that the quantum world declares them to be the leaders of their own lives so that instead of being a victim of their circumstances because of their thought level, they can become participators in creating new circumstances. Then 'the led' will know that they can ask: 'what shall we collectively create?' When strong leaders are operating at a values-only level, they will have three characteristics: they will lead by example, they will consistently champion the values they espouse, and their key decisions will be values-driven. When strong leaders are operating at a spiritual level, they will consider their leadership from a position of being, not doing, and it is 'Only when the choice to serve undergirds the moral formation of the leader that the hierarchical power that separates the leader and those led does not corrupt.'[107] The spiritually intelligent leader is driven by a passion to serve, and not by the pursuit of status, power and conspicuous accomplishment.

Leaders are a 'living values system' and they are leading a living value-system – the organisation. The nature of each of these as well as their relationship becomes clearer and clearer as the spirit of the leader develops. 'Without this avenue of spiritual development, the leader is likely to experience little more than a cacophony of competing priorities and constraints, both inside the self and outside in the organisation and the wider environment.'[108] When all is said and done, the great leader will be 'first experienced as a servant to others, and this simple fact is central to his or her greatness.'[109]

And so, executive development for leaders leading spiritually intelligent people must be about spiritual development.

- *Importance of role models*
  The sixteenth century Newtonian model of the world (which states that all that exists is what can be experienced by the five senses and that everything is separate) has governed our view of what success is. Success is measured by sensory indicators such as results, wealth (in 1996, 447 billionaires had a net worth equal to the combined income of the poorest half of the world's population), power, looks and associating with people who are demonstrating these sensory indicators. Television and cinema have done a lot to promulgate this model of success by providing many role models who reflect all or some of the sensory indicators. What's more, the Newtonian model of the world tells us that we are all separate from one another and from Nature so that what we do in order to be successful will not impact on others or Nature.

  This model creates a self-focussed success. Quantum physics on the other hand has discovered that the Newtonian model is not how the world operates; that mankind functions in a sea of intelligence – 'the electron sea' as physicist David Bohm calls it; that this sea of intelligence is a 'unified field' of which each of us is a part and each 'thing' is a part and so, in fact, we are all connected – humans, things, Nature; that our thoughts affect this unified field and, therefore, everyone and everything. So, the model of success based on the Newtonian model of the world is seriously flawed and cannot provide long-term success but only long-term damage.

  Many writers[110] have identified that all thought processes come from one of two origins – fear or love – and that fear-based decisions and actions are damaging to the whole while love-based decisions are constructive to the whole. These writers have also examined the processes/crises that individuals have to go through to crack wide open and slough off that part of themselves that allows fear in – namely their ego and cultural biases. They have documented that once this process is well underway, these individuals have access to their central core (their spirit); are able to tap into their intuition and are able to connect with a Higher Intelligence (God/Source) and receive instructions and guidance from that Intelligence. Consequently, they are more astute, more strategic – being aware of all factors involved in a situation and aware of the bigger picture; they are more 'win-win' because the nature of that Higher Intelligence is constructive, not destructive and they are able to connect with other people at a core level, i.e. they can by-pass the 'dross elements' in someone and connect with who that person truly is – energy to energy/spirit to spirit. So, they are inspirational.

These individuals are functioning in harmony with the true nature of the design of our earth system and have learned how to create using their words, thoughts and intentions. As Deepak Chopra reminds us, 'in thought are the mechanics of the fulfilment of that thought.'[111] So, these people have learned what success is in the quantum model: a constructive mind set knowing that thought is powerful; being win-win and working for the good of all; taking time to help others appreciate that we have moved on from the sixteenth century and that our physicists today have a different view of the mechanisms that govern our world; helping others apply these principles to the task in hand, i.e. being what Greenleaf calls 'a servant leader'. This leader can enjoy the trappings of success found in the Newtonian model, but does not need them: they own the trappings rather than the trappings owning them. However, the pull in our modern world to be a leader from the Newtonian model is very strong. So there is an urgent need for aspiring and experienced managers and leaders to be trained in the quantum model of leadership and in how to transform their organisations so that they will be a reflection of that ethos.

- *The learning organisation*
  Relevance in today's changing world requires accessing feedback and acting on that feedback. To be relevant, today's workplace must be in a constant learning mode: employees must learn new skills, learn about new products; organisations must learn about more appropriate structures, leading and management. But, as I have already mentioned, downsizing has placed demands on employees to have inner, personal skills to cope with the effects of downsizing, not least the stress of an increased workload, the stress of a forthcoming lay-off or the fear of long-term unemployment. One man who understands well the practical application of the quantum model to the workplace is organisational development expert, writer and speaker, Peter Senge.[112] Peter Senge has created a model for organisations to keep themselves relevant – a learning organisation model – based on the practice of five disciplines: systems thinking; personal mastery (understanding personal capacities and dreams); mental models (examining and overturning redundant, destructive, narrow or limiting personal beliefs); shared vision (building a collective dream to guide future action); and team learning (collaborating to work and develop the intellectual, emotional and spiritual talent of team members in small groups). Each of these disciplines has an element based on ego and an element based on spirit. Peter Senge's work aims to redress the balance of these two elements because, as he points out, most organisations have leaned too heavily on the 'ego' side.

- *Inspiring activities / events / objects*
  Spiritually intelligent organisations understand the importance of creating activities, events that are inspirational. They do not leave this to chance. Many people have been to a match or concert that has been so uplifting that they spoke about it for days. The astonishingly inspirational effect of Riverdance at the Eurovision Song Contest some years ago, or even the current series of Riverdance shows running throughout the US and Europe, is an example of how deeply affected and uplifted people can be by an activity or event. The psychologists Myers and Briggs[113] identified in their research that 75% of the Western populace is affected psychologically by their physical environment. This is why inspiring objects strategically placed around the workplace, as well as the use of colours chosen for the psychological benefits they will have on the viewer, are so important.

- *Paid time off for community work*
  There are limits to how far the organisation itself can inspire and give meaning to its employees. Some enlightened organisations have been providing their employees with paid time off during company hours to do voluntary work in their local communities. This has caused employees to find personal fulfilment and, therefore, bring greater motivation back to the job. They also feel that the organisation is supporting them in being of service and making a difference.

Spiritual intelligence in the workplace has meant that organisations are structuring work so that it is fulfilling, enjoyable and productive.

(7) **Work environment externally supportive of spirituality**
Given that quantum physics has educated mankind about the

operating mechanisms of the planet; that people throughout the Western world are clearly educating themselves about the inner realm of the spirit; and given that many companies have engaged in exploring spiritual intelligence in their workplaces, it would seem that Western consciousness has evolved to the point that it is ready to wholly and openly explore the practical application of spirituality in business and government. The Japanese Science Council has suggested that there will be many crises to be overcome in this century and that all levels of society and organisations in Japan 'must uphold the ideal of contributing to all of humanity and to the planet and must urge the international community to strive for global solidarity.'[114]

What does an organisation that is supportive of spirituality look like? It is one that is socially responsible and whose current actions will not adversely affect future generations. It is one that looks after all its relationships – with suppliers, customers, employees, and community. And it is aware that it is not just the organisation that defines the stakeholder. For example, Disney has promised one million hours of voluntary service from its employees to a mentoring program for children at risk in city areas. K-Mart will allow its 2,150 stores to be used as safe havens for children at risk. Nike has created 'Zone Parks' in primary school play grounds to tackle bullying – and they are successful. Coca-Cola has pledged money to train volunteers to act as mentors to disadvantaged children and has distributed thousands of leaflets in Africa on Aids.

The work environment externally supportive of spirituality knows that there may be stakeholders out there who have not been considered by the company and yet define or reject the company as a stakeholder (for example people living in an area being polluted by an organisation, nations living near another nation, one of whose industries is creating pollution affecting a geographic spread beyond its borders). The organisation externally supportive of spirituality practises servant leadership and asks 'Do our stakeholders grow as persons: do they, while being served, become healthier, wiser, freer, more autonomous, more likely themselves to become servants?' It asks 'What is the effect on the least privileged in society? Will s/he benefit or at least not be further deprived?'[115] It makes sure that no one will knowingly be hurt directly or indirectly by any activity undertaken by the company. This type of organisation often gives 10% of pre-tax profits to philanthropic groups (e.g. The Huntsman Chemical Corporation in Utah with 10,000 employees has donated $100 million of its profit to a cancer centre at the University of Utah and has built a concrete plant in Armenia to house those rendered homeless by the 1988 earthquake) and may even run public seminars and/or conferences on the topic of spirituality in the workplace.

One example of this is the international conference that took place at the World Bank in Washington DC on 23 October 1995. Not only did this conference stimulate discussion among many organisations on the subject, but it opened up the way for the subject to be discussed at the Bank. Another outcome from the conference was the setting up of the Spiritual Unfoldment Society (SUS) at the Bank. The aim of SUS is to 'encourage the integration of higher consciousness into every aspect of our lives... and to create within the World Bank a consciousness of love and understanding that contributes towards transforming the way we interact with one another (and the way the organisation interacts with the world).'[116] Another example is the International Christian Chamber of Commerce based in Sweden with more than 80 national chapters. The ICCC launched a ten-week video series in China called *You Can Start Your Own Business*. China asked the ICCC to develop the course, which would be aired over their public broadcasting television system that has a potential audience of over 250,000 million viewers. China first interviewed Microsoft and IBM for this project. However, their determining factor in selecting ICCC was their emphasis on ethics.[117] In 1986, The Caux Round table, based in Minnesota, 'pioneered a list of Principles for Business, an international code of business values formulated by senior business leaders from Japan, Europe and the United States and Canada. They endorsed a concept presented by the CEO of the Japanese-based Canon company called 'kyosei', which means 'working together for the common good and sharing prosperity.'[118]

(8) The national/political aspects of spirituality in the workplace

Set against a backdrop of horrific pollution in its capital city, over one thousand earthquakes (6+ on the Richter Scale) on its southern coasts in 2000, enormously long working days, a frighteningly high suicide rate and a faltering economy, Japan has issued a 'Life-Work-Education' document aimed to bring balance back onto its shores. Produced by the Japanese Science Council, which comprises eminent professors from the nation's top universities, the document advocates the need for new value systems and new lifestyles of 'self-sufficiency and reduced prosperity based on respect for life and an appreciation of life's diversity as well as systems for re-circulating and re-cycling earth's resources.' They have also planned a spiritual education designed to encourage a 'recognition of human dignity and self-worth and grounded in the history of the human race and scientific knowledge.' The Council has planned to create 'new lifestyle industries' to provide the driving force for the transition from consumerism towards a lifestyle not based on materialism and the use of polluting fuels.[119] However, such a lifestyle transformation will take time to achieve especially if other Western countries do not take up a similar stance. Yet, the Kyoto agreement is an example of countries looking at a more holistic approach to managing the global environment.

(9) Spiritual intelligence in the workplace: techniques

There are some strongly religious techniques emerging in the workplace, such as prayer groups, meditation, daily rituals, theological disciplines, daily scripture and contemplation, including an internet version of these via sites such as the Microsoft online prayer site, beliefnet.com, sites offering Buddhist, Hindu, Muslim, Jewish and Christian scripture readings every day, and the Jesuit.ie/prayer site which offers a ten minute meditation including thoughts to contemplate, a scripture and prayer.

Some companies like Tom's of Maine bring in spiritual leaders – from divinity school professors to Native American tribal elders – to speak to employees regularly. Some of these leaders serve on the Tom's of Maine Board. Other companies have engaged in more secular but employee-centred approaches: more flexible hours, more job-sharing opportunities, support for employees' volunteer work outside the company, child- and elder-care support, compassionate response to worker stress, social workers/psychotherapists/chaplains to support employees' emotional and spiritual needs (this technique alone has brought Marriot International a 418% rate of return on its investment in terms of reduced absenteeism, better quality work and improved relationships among employees),[120] gender and ethnic inclusion practices, exercise of social responsibility in the wider community, and building strategic alliances with the local community.

Many companies have engaged in training programmes, using hypnosis, guided visualisation, thought management, colour therapy, music therapy, sound therapy, aromatherapy, mountain climbing, sweat lodges, dialogue, and massage.

(10) Research
A 'spiritual audit' of corporate America, conducted for publishers Jossey-Bass by Ian Mitroff (who holds the Harold Quinton Distinguished Professorship of Business Policy at the Marshall School of Business at the University of Southern California in Los Angeles) and Elizabeth Denton (an independent organisational consultant based in New York City

and working for Fortune 100 companies and entrepreneurial companies) in 1999 is a very thorough audit using a comprehensive 50-question questionnaire. Such a study would be interesting to carry out in several countries that reflect different cultural expressions from that of the US. Obviously, much of the literature on the subject of spirituality in the workplace is from the US and expresses that country's methods of coping with the ways in which national and corporate culture have affected human beings there. However, because US companies have sited themselves in virtually every European country and brought their cultures into those sites, many European companies may not be that far off the findings of Mitroff and Denton. What will be valuable is a study of non-US companies vis-à-vis spirituality.

(11) Obstacles

Several obstacles exist to bringing spiritual intelligence into the workplace: discomfort/fear among board members, management and employees in broaching the subject; training events not really hitting the mark and so coming across as meaningless; investor resistance, separating life and work and, therefore, not seeing the relevance of the subject; and lack of know-how.

Notes

1. Gregg Braden, *Awakening to Zero Point* (Bellevue, WA: Radio Bookstore Press, 1997), pp. 32-39
2. The Holy Bible, New King James Version (Nashville: Thomas Nelson Publishers), Galatians Chapter 5 v.22
3. Dalai Lama, *Ethics for a New Millennium* (Riverhead Books, 1999)
4. Ian I. Mitroff and Elizabeth Denton, *A Spiritual Audit of Corporate America* (San Francisco, CA: Jossey-Bass Inc., 1999), p. xvii
5. Danah Zohar and Ian Marshall, *SQ: Connecting with our Spiritual Intelligenc* (NY: Bloomsbury Publishing, 2000), p. 6
6. Francis Fukuyama, *Trust: The Social Virtues and the Creation of Prosperity* (London: Penguin Books, 1995), p. 5
7. Zohar and Marshall, p. 159

8.   Ibid., p.112
9.   Ibid., p. 9
10. Deepak Chopra, *New Physics of Healing* [Audio Cassette] (Boulder, CO: Sounds True Recordings, 1990)
11. F. Varela, E. Thompson and E. Rosch, *The Embodied Mind: Cognitive Science and Human Experience* (Cambridge: MIT Press, 1991)
12. Wayne W. Dyer, *Manifest Your Destiny* (London: Thorsons, 1998)
13. Chopra, op. cit.
14. Ibid.
15. Ibid.
16. Alain Aspect, www.sheldrake.org/experiments/pigeons
17. Rupert Sheldrake, *The Presence of the Past: Morphic Resonance and the Habits of Nature* (Inner Traditions, 1995)
18. David Bohn, *The Special Theory of Relativity* (Routledge, 1996)
19. Candace B. Pert, *Molecules of Emotion* (London: Simon and Schuster, 1998)
20. James Moravec, 'Spiritual Perspectives in the Workplace,' www.urantiabook.org/archive/sfj/workplace.htm
21. Chopra, op. cit.
22. Zohar and Marshall, op. cit., pp. 123-164
23. Mitroff and Denton, op. cit., p. xv
24. Kahlil Gibran, *The Prophet* (New York: Alfred A. Knopf, 1997)
25. St Teresa of Avila, *The Interior Castle,* edited by Halcyon Backhouse (London: Hodder & Stoughton, 1988)
26. Tara Fenwick and Elizabeth Lange, 'The Turn To The Spiritual in Workplace Training and Development', www.ualberta.ca/~tfenwick/ext/spirit.htm
27. Zohar and Marshall, op. cit., pp. 225-259
28. Roger Harrison, *Organization Culture and Quality of Service* (London: Association of Management Education & Development, 1987), pp. 18-19
29. B. Cohen and J. Greenfield, 'Ben & Jerry's Double Dip: Lead with Your Values and Make Money, Too (New York: Simon & Schuster, 1997), pp. 51-52
30. Zohar and Marshall, op. cit., p. 239
31. Joseph Jaworski, op. cit., p. 128
32. Zohar and Marshall, op. cit., p. 90
33. Butch Farley, 'Corporate Spirituality It's An Inside Job,' www.todayscoach.com/April2001/workplace.htm

34. Daniel Goleman, *Emotional Intelligence* (London: Bloomsbury Publishing, 1996)
35. Robert K. Greenleaf, *The Power of Servant Leadership* (San Francisco, CA: Berrett-Koehler Publishers, 1998), p. 7
36. Mitroff and Denton, op. cit., p. xv
37. Richard Barrett, *Liberating the Corporate Soul* (USA: Butterworth-Heinemann, 1998); Zohar and Marshall, op. cit.; Frederick G. Harmon, *Playing for Keeps* (New York & Toronto : John Wiley & Sons, 1996); Michele Hunt, *Dream Makers* (Palo Alto, CA: Davies-Black, 1998)
38. Corinne McLaughlin, 'Spirituality in Business', World Goodwill Occasional Paper, April 1999, p. 2
39. Richard C Whiteley, Harvard Business School [Bulletin Online], www.alumni.hbs.edu/buttetin/1999/april/spirit.html
40. Richard Barrett, op. cit., p. 3
41. Joseph Jaworski, *Synchronicity* (San Francisco, CA: Berrett-Koehler, 1996), p. 130
42. Alice Mack, 'Secular Spirituality: A New Vision for the Workplace & Beyond', www.personal.riverusers.com/~amack/spirit.html
43. Robert Quinn, *Change the World* (San Francisco: Jossey-Bass, 2000), p. 69
44. Tanis Helliwell, *Take Your Soul to Work* (Adams Business Media, 2000)
45. Matthew Fox, *The Reinvention of Work* (San Francisco: Harper, 1995)
46. Gregg Levoy, *Callings* (Three Rivers, 1998)
47. Richard Barrett, op. cit., p. 151
48. Robert Quinn, op. cit., p. 65
49. Mitroff and Denton, op. cit., p. 36
50. Peter A Vaill, *Spirited Leading and Learning* (San Francisco, CA: Jossey-Bass, 1998), p. 179
51. 'Spirituality in My Workplace?! Not that God Talk!' www.worksalive.com/articles.html
52. Dyer, op. cit., 1998
53. 'Spirituality in My Workplace?! Not that God Talk! www.worksalive.com/articles.html
54. Ibid.
55. Alan L. Pritz, 'Spirituality in the Workplace: A New Business Dynamic,' www.innerresourceenhancement.com/spirituality_workplace.htm

56. *God Calling* (New Jersey: Jove Publications for Fleming H. Revell Co., 1981), p. 129

57. The Holy Bible, New King James Version, Psalm 46, v.5

58. Joseph Jaworski, op. cit., p. 12

59. James Moravec, 'Spiritual Perspectives in the Workplace,' www.urantiabook.org/archive/sfj/workplace.htm

60. Zohar and Marshall, op. cit., p. 156

61. Vaill, op. cit., p. 216

62. Heather Joy Skelton, 'Spirituality in the Workplace,' www.aliveworks.com/Article_spirit.htm

63. Jaworski, op. cit., p. 179

64. Zohar and Marshall, op. cit., p. 238

65. Chris Argyris, 'Crafting a Theory of Practice: The Case of Organizational Paradoxes', in R. Quinn and K. Cameron (eds), *Paradox and Transformation* (Cambridge, Mass: Ballinger, 1988)

66. Quinn (2000), op. cit., pp. 84-86

67. Ibid, pp. 67, 90

68. Jaworski, op. cit., p. 140

69. Thomas Hamblin, *His Wisdom Guiding* (Sussex, UK: The Science of Thought Press, 1979), p. 94

70. Abraham Maslow, *Toward a Psychology of Being* (New York: Van Nostrand Reinhold, 1982)

71. Quinn (2000), op. cit., p. 88

72. Susan Jeffers, *Feel The Fear and Do It Anyway* (Fawcett Books, 1992)

73. Robert Greenleaf, *Servant Leadership: A Journey into the Nature of Legitimate Power and Greatness* (New York: Paulist Press, 1977), Chapter 11

74. Mitroff and Denton, op. cit., p. 47

75. Joseph Campbell, *The Hero with a Thousand Faces* (Princeton, NJ: Princeton University Press, 1949)

76. Mitroff and Denton, op. cit., pp. 57-163

77. Margaret Wheatley, *Leadership and the New Science* (San Francisco, CA: Berrett-Koehler Publishers, 1999)

78. Vaill, op. cit., p. 196

79. Heather Skelton, 'Spirituality in the Workplace,' www.omegactr.com/source/spirwork.htm.

80. Viktor E. Frankl, *Man's Search for Meaning* (Washington: Washington Square, 1998)

81. Pert, op. cit.

82. Deepak Chopra, *Magical Mind Magical Body* [Audio Cassettes] (Nighingate Conant Corp.) Tape 1 & 6

83. Wayne W. Dyer, *You'll See It When You Believe It* (Avon, 1990)

84. Barrett, op. cit., pp. xv, 212

85. Martin Rutte, 'Spirituality in the Workplace,' www.martinrutte.com/heart.html

86. David Dorsey, 'The New Spirit of Work,' www.fastcompany.com/online/16/barrett.html

87. Corinne McLaughlin, 'Spirituality in the Workplace,' www.walkerinternational.com/article63.html

88. Fukuyama, op. cit., p. 9

89. Harmon, op. cit., p. 16

90. www.itstime.com/rainbow.htm

91. Mitroff and Denton, op. cit., p. 127

92. Ibid, p. 52

93. Albert Mehrabian, *Basic Behaviour Modification* (Human Sciences Pr., 1978)

94. Tara Fenwick and Elizabeth Lang, www.ualberta.ca/~tfenwick/ext/spirit.htm

95. Malcolm Simpkin, Virgin Direct, 'Flair and Passion versus Structure and Control'; CSM Focus Event, Edinburgh, 10 November 1999

96. Jaworski, op. cit., Preface

97. Fukuyama, op. cit., p. 6

98. Alfie Kohn, 'How Incentives Undermine Performance,' *Journal of Quality and Participation*, March/April 1998, pp. 7-13

99. Fukuyama, op. cit., p. 360

100. M. Csikszentmihalyi, *Finding Flow: The Psychology of Engagement with Everyday Life* (New York: Basic Book, 1997), pp. 88-89

101. Pert, op. cit.

102. George Land and Beth Jarman, *Breaking Point and Beyond* (San Francisco: HarperBusiness, 1993) p. 153

103. Rosabeth Moss Kanter, *The Change Masters* (Simon & Schuster, 1985)

104. Arie De Geus, *The Living Company: Habits for Survival in a Turbulent Business Environment* (Boston: Harvard Business School Press, 1997)

105. Joseph Campbell, op. cit., 1949

106. Zohar and Marshall, op. cit., p. 239

107. Jaworski, op. cit., p. 1

108. Vaill, op. cit., p. 227

109. Robert Greenleaf (1988), op. cit., p. 4
110. Vera Peiffer, *Positively Fearless* (Rockport, MA: Element Inc., 1993), Dorothy Rowe, *Beyond Fear* (London: Fontana, 1987), Susan Jeffers, *End the Struggle and Dance With Life: How to Build Yourself Up When the World Get You Down* (London: Hodder & Stoughton, 1996), Bob Mandel, *Open Heart Therapy* (Berkeley, CA: Celestial Arts Publishing, 1984)
111. Chopra (1990), op. cit.
112. Peter M. Senge, *The Fifth Discipline* (London: Century Business, 1993)
113. David Keirsey and Marilyn Bates, *Please Understand Me* (Del Mar, CA: Prometheus Nemesis Book Company, 1978)
114. Science Council of Japan, 'Towards a Comprehensive Solution to Problems in Education and the Environment based on a Recognition of Human Dignity and Self-Worth', July 2000
115. Robert Greenleaf (1998), op. cit. p. 43
116. Richard Barrett, 'Spiritual Unfolding At The World Bank,' www.corptools.com/text/spiritun.htm
117. Os Hillman, 'Spirituality In The Workplace,' www.wowi.net/articles/articlesvw.cgi?command=view&id=752rnd=162.6741323 6177964
118. Corinne McLaughlin, 'Spirituality in the Workplace,' www.walkerinternational.com/article63.html
119. Science Council of Japan
120. *Washington Post*, 1 October 1995, 'Workplace' by Kristin Downay Grimsley

CHAPTER III

HOW TO BRING SPIRITUAL INTELLIGENCE INTO YOUR WORKPLACE

If there is light in the soul,
There will be beauty in the person.

If there is beauty in the person,
There will be harmony in the house.

If there is harmony in the house,
There will be order in the nation.

If there is order in the nation,
There will be peace in the world.
– Chinese Proverb

There are several questions that can be asked to prompt the birth and growth of spiritual intelligence in your workplace: questions that relate to spirituality generally; questions relating to the individual person; questions relating to leadership; and questions relating to the organisation. There are also some actions that individuals, leaders and organisations can take to spark spiritual intelligence. We shall look firstly at the questions in detail.

- Questions that Relate to Spirituality Generally

  - When does the spirit of employees become subdued and overshadowed?
  - Is your organisation a dispiriting place?
  - Are there leaders in your organisation who are dispiriting, whose impact blocks the spirit of others/sours the climate of the organisation?
  - What disincentives are there in your company to discussing spirituality?
  - Is there someone in your company that is developed enough spiritually to head up a project on spiritual intelligence in your organisation?

- Questions that Relate to the Individual Person

  - Have you any stored-up images, interpretations, feelings, doubts, distrusts, likes and dislikes (filters/mental maps) that situations, things or people evoke in you?
  - Are you aware that you are looking at life through the filters of the above?
  - Are you aware of the filters that others have?
  - Are you able to deal with others without judging them? (Which does not mean that you do not give the feedback they must have. Judgement is about your disposition, that inner feeling you have about someone/something.)
  - What are your filters/mental maps about the meaning of life, how the world operates, your country, your nationality, your religion?
  - Have you reflected on your filters/mental maps in a group situation, listening to others' and sharing your own?

- In such a group situation, did you feel that you wanted to judge the other person for having the views they have?
- Have you undertaken self-development and awareness training?
- Do you ask yourself, when you are in a situation and with people – especially new situations and people – 'How does this help me understand truth?' and 'How does this add meaning to my life?'
- Have you considered the best experience you have ever had in an organisation – the most memorable – and what that felt like and how you could re-create those feelings in the present moment?
- What are your feelings about who you are, what you are doing, what contributions you are making to life, your family, your society, your company?
- What gives you the most meaning and purpose in your job?
- How much and which parts of yourself are you able to express at work?
- List the basic values that govern your life.
- Are you acting in congruence with your values?
- Do you regularly ask 'why'?
- Do you look for connections between things/situations/people?
- Do you choose how you will respond in a situation, or just react?
- How much do you know about yourself?
- Do other people tell you about aspects of yourself that you were either unaware of or strongly disagreed with?
- Are you honest with yourself?
- Do you ever blame yourself or others?
- How do you express your creativity at work?
- Are 'truth' seekers drawn to you by the way you conduct yourself in and out of the workplace?

- Are you in your organisation because you choose to be there or because you feel you have no other option?
- Do you often feel that you get the 'raw end of the stick'?
- Do you treat each experience as an opportunity for growth?
- Are you aware of websites that can give you development tips for your personal growth such as www.topten.org which offers regular 'top ten ways' to manage yourself and www.beliefnet.com which offers inspirational articles?

• Questions that Relate to Leadership

- Are you aware that just being there for others and listening to them is one of the most important capacities a leader can have?
- Do you allow your people to express fully what is in them?
- Are you aware of your employees' hopes, concerns, fears, pain?
- Do you allow your employees (male and female) to share their feelings with you? And do you treat their feelings as important?
- Are you aware that a low level of trust in your organisation is an indicator of the fact that employees feelings and thoughts are being repressed, i.e. that the organisation is emotionally unintelligent?
- Have you been through an 'emotional intelligence' programme?
- Do you respond actively to another's needs and concerns and give help and assistance when it is not your job?
- Do you give credit for employees' ideas and build on their contributions?
- Are you generous with your trust, i.e. do you give employees the benefit of the doubt?

- Do you see your employees as valuable and unique in themselves and not simply for their contribution to the task?
- Do you nurture the growth of your employees, i.e. teach, support, encourage, smooth their path?
- Are you aware that the more time you spend helping employees grow and develop, the more successful the organisation will be?
- Do you look for the good and the positive in others and acknowledge it when you find it?
- Do those you lead grow as persons?
- Under your leadership, do your people become healthier, wiser, freer, more autonomous, and more likely to reflect spiritual intelligence?
- Do you see your organisation as a living or inanimate system?
- Are you responsive and responsible to the needs of your organisation as a living system?
- The chief communicator of values is always the behaviour of the leader of the unit. Are you walking the talk?
- Are you aware that whenever there is a gap between expectation and performance, definitions of values must change?
- Do you take time to define for employees what exactly the company values mean to your unit now?
- Do you get out and about among your employees, colleagues and customers to listen to what they have to say?
- Do you see failure in your employees as a learning opportunity or as a failure?
- Are you aware that failure must be seen as a learning opportunity if creativity and innovation is to be nurtured?
- Are you aware of the power of your stories to influence your people?

- What opportunities can you give to your people for them to express their creativity?
- Are you aware that your inner model never mirrors reality – that it is always a construct?
- Do you regularly give yourself the opportunity to re-perceive reality by having scenario-based discussions with people from varied walks of life?
- Do you use the process of dialogue in which an agenda-less sharing of views is held in order to obtain deeper meaning in a situation?
- How would you go about creating a department that has a spiritual focus?

• Questions that Relate to the Organisation

- Do corporate values influence and energise every process?
- Has your organisation decided what kind of company it wants to be, what kind of company it does not want to be, what it wants its employees to say about it and what it wants to be known for in the broader community within which it operates?
- Does the company regularly review its values definitions of the needs and wants of customers and employees?
- When values definitions change, do structures and systems change with them also so that there is congruence within the organisation?
- Does the organisation understand 'the various elements of values not in isolation but as a whole taken together and that no subsets of values in the value system can be substituted for the whole system without altering its character'?[1]
- Has the organisation created a culture that supports personal growth?
- Has the organisation considered offering paid volunteer work as an employee perk?

- Has the organisation built a culture of employee participation and institutionalised the search for innovation?
- Has the company taken seriously its responsibility to build among its employees a strong sense of community?
- Has the company created the conditions that support sociability (genuine friendliness) and solidarity (the ability to pursue shared objectives quickly and efficiently)?
- Has the company worked to eliminate boundaries?
- Is the organisation aware that cultural compatibility is more important in the long term than hiring or promoting excellent technical people who cannot build trust, empower others or create internal cohesion?
- How does the way work is organised affect employees' personal lives?
- How can changes in the way work is done positively affect both business outcomes and employees' lives?
- Does the organisation have a training schedule to support its culture?
- What new forms of education are required to develop your organisation and members, especially in non-coercive ways?
- Does the company regularly ask 'Why are we doing things the way we are?'
- Is your organisation aware that it urgently needs to ask 'at this critical point in history not whether is should become more spiritual but rather how it can.'?[2]
- Is the organisation aware of what people consider offensive with regard to spirituality?
- How can the organisation promote spirituality without sanctioning religion?
- What crisis/crises have your organisation had that highlight that it needs to move to a higher ethical plane if it is to avoid future crises?

- What forms of denial have prevented your organisation from recognising the crises that have happened to it?
- What are the previous principles by which the organisation has been run that have led it to the brink of crisis and prevented it from being more ethical?
- How can such principles be countered?
- What new sources of knowledge and wisdom does your organisation need to draw on in order to move to a higher ethical and spiritual plane?
- How does your organisation intend to consider the well-being of future generations?
- Has the organisation produced a visionary focus for its people that excites them and causes them to want to put in their own energy?
- Does the organisation allow manufacturing staff (who usually have to remain in a limited space for long periods) exercise breaks?
- Does the company stage frequent celebrations to acknowledge milestones and achievements?
- Does the company 'honour and encourage creative expression by decorating the workplace with employee-made paintings, sculpture, craft work and poetry?'[3]
- If your company participates in trade shows, does it rotate those it allows to attend and include not just the personnel directly related to the show?
- Does your company encourage employees to get to know each other as people as well as the functions they fulfil?
- Does your company assist new employees to integrate well and quickly into their new workplace?
- What does your company do to create a sense of connectedness for new employees?
- Does your organisation help employees connect with nature by bringing in as many natural features as possible – green plants, skylights, fountains, full-spectrum

lighting (which gives the same light as daylight and improves productivity and psychological well-being) and ionisers (which charge the air with good ions. There are 100,000 good ions – called negative ions – per cubic foot by the sea or in the mountains. There are only 100 good ions per cubic foot in an office in the city or on a production floor in the city)?
- Does your company encourage the policy of holding meetings outdoors whenever weather permits?

• Personal Action Items

To stimulate spiritual intelligence within yourself, you can:
- meditate;
- slow down the pace by listening to relaxing music (there are pieces of music specially designed to de-stress, induce sleep, induce creativity, even to manufacture neural networks in the brain)[4];
- slow down the pace by going for a walk where you will get peace to think, for example, by the beach, in the woods, in the hills, in the mountains, along country lanes;
- have a little book in which you document what has been good about each day/what was beautiful that day/what instances of love and compassion you experienced that day/what instances of abundance you experienced that day/how you managed to overcome an old thought or behaviour pattern/what you could have done differently/what you have learned that day.

• Leadership Action Items

To spark spiritual intelligence in your people try:
- communicating to your people that you believe they matter and that you know they have something important to give;

- strengthening the self-belief and confidence of your people;
- asking your people to identify the critical acts that make up a job, to find ways to add more value to the way they carry out each of those critical acts, to work out ways to measure the team's progress on these critical acts and to set up a regular review system that monitors progress on how well the 'value-addedness' is happening on those critical acts;
- encouraging your people to rely on their inner resources that they may not be tapping, to use their intuition, to be innovative and improvise in the face of uncertainty, ambiguity, and when the goal-posts change;
- building deep trust and respect among your people;
- helping each of your people clear out their limiting and narrow belief systems;
- helping your team experience that 'flow state' that occurs in all real teams;
- providing development training for your people and for yourself that will put you each in a situation that forces you to dig deeply inside of yourself in order to connect with your spiritual core;
- providing development training for your people and for yourself that teaches you to be open to continuous transformation so that, like the chameleon, you can adapt quickly to change and to new environments.
- building your business on relationships. A failed business is a failed relationship;
- checking in with your employees to see how they are doing, how their family is, how they felt about news items;
- understanding that a core competence of your function is to manage energy – the energy of your people – and to serve others, and that if you do that, your people will work with maximum effectiveness, and so meet their financial targets;

- making work fun: have dress up days (as in fancy dress) or comedy days;
- giving your employees a larger vision: support charities/causes that they feel strongly about and get the whole team involved;
- holding regular 'what if' sessions, asking your Team what should be started, stopped, continued;
- teaching your people about the 'unified field', that it makes everything out of its invisible energy, that the only problems are the negative, fearful, narrow beliefs that vie for our attention and that a fundamental aspect of their 'job' is to stay in tune with their spiritual core and keep theirs constructive – even in demanding circumstances.

- Organisational Action Plan

You can help stimulate spiritual intelligence in your organisation by running workshops in:
- intuition;
- meditation;
- creative visualisation;
- deep breathing to reduce stress and bring individuals to their spiritual centre;
- shared values;
- active, deep listening;
- making action and intention congruent;
- tai chi (for production workers particularly);
- creativity;
- diversity management;
- dialogue (as opposed to discussion) skills.

You can also provide mentors for those who are ready for the 'inner journey'.

Notes

1. Peter B. Vaill, *Spirited Leading and Learning* (San Francisco, CA: Jossey-Bass Inc. Pub., 1998), p. 225

2. Ian I. Mitroff and Elizabeth Denton, *A Spiritual Audit of Corporate America* (San Francisco, CA: Jossey-Bass Inc. Pub., 1999) p. 168

3. *HR Magazine*, April 1996, Tom's of Maine, 'Eleven Steps To a More Spiritual Company',
    www.shrm.org/hrmagazine/articles/default.asp?page=0496toms.htm

4. Mind Aerobics (by The New You Enterprises, 4470 SW Hall Blvd Suite 163 Beaverton OR 97005) and *Solitudes, Music for Your Health* (Manufactured and distributed by Solitudes Ltd., 1131A Leslie St Suite 500 Toronto, Canada M3C 3L8, distributed in the USA by The Direct Company, Box 327, Botsford, CT 06404)

CHAPTER IV

DANGERS

Only insecure people need security.
Secure people know there is no such thing.
Security comes from within,
When you know you can handle anything.
– Wayne Dyer

A huge overgrown bush, with a thick and massive undergrowth, and a deep and complex rooting system, describes the ego structure that has been seeded, fertilised, nurtured and cultivated in Western organisations. For the plants that were originally placed beside the now overgrown bush, the fact that this huge bush has been left to grow in such an unruly and free manner has meant that they are not even visible – in fact, some would say they don't even exist. But they are there. We are affected at a deeper and less visible manner than our personalities by our culture, and at an even deeper and less visible level again by the spiritual codes to which we have been exposed. The Reticular Activating System (RAS) in the brain only lets us see what matches our belief systems, but to get a belief, it takes exposure to that belief of one hour per day over a period of twenty one days.[1] If a person has been operating for years at the ego level, then all his/her RAS will allow him/her to see is life through the filter of his/her personality and the value system and behaviours that go with the ego level. This value system exhorts the individual to look after 'number one' (self) and typical behaviours would be games, posturings, playing roles, negative politicking, obsession with power and control, being overly self-conscious, overly rational, obsessive *vis-à-vis* partialities of one's personality, e.g. obsessive with detail/anarchy/wheeling and dealing/ empathising with people. Mired in so many layers of limiting 'software', it is very difficult for someone at this most superficial of levels to even grasp that they *are* at a superficial level and that there are deeper levels from which to live life.

Draped in the colours of their national flag, steeped in the traditions of their country, yet developed enough to have learned that their own personality type is not the only one, and so they must learn the art of looking at life from the view of the other personality types, is the person engulfed by their national culture. My country may consist of mainly white-skinned people and I may not realise that I have an antipathy towards black/brown-skinned people. My country's religion may be of only one persuasion and I may resist those from other countries who practise a different religious persuasion. Once again, my RAS will not let me see that this is going on because it exists to show me *only* what matches my belief systems, and to throw out everything else.

It is usually only after a crisis – and normally after a protracted period of many long dark nights of the soul, facing fear, anxiety, isolation, disillusion, desolation and despair – that a person finally comes to live from their spiritual core. No more does their personality get in the way, or the behaviours of a sturdy ego; no more do the boundaries created by nationalist thinking and culture block the reaching out to help another; no more does fear affect thinking and decision-making. At this level, the individual acts according to conscience – even if that involves personal risk and his/her actions and decisions are based on universal principles.

But, this stage is not arrived at after one or two training courses – not even with a degree! This stage has to be hard earned and the coin is pain.

* * *

So, my first concern about a project bringing spiritual intelligence into the workplace is that it may only function at one of the more superficial levels. Another concern is that unless it is facilitated by people who are already functioning from their spiritual core, the organisation can only hope to experience spiritual intelligence at the level of the facilitator. It is also part of the human condition to avoid pain and move towards pleasure. The wonderful work of Joe Grinder and Richard Bandler[2] has proven this. So, not too many people at work will want to add any further pain into their lives by going through a deep spiritual journey. With the fluctuations of the global economy, and tens of thousands of jobs regularly in danger in the Western world, there is enough pain in considering how the mortgage is to be paid! This means that if organisations really want to reap the financial and social benefits of having an organisation functioning from the spiritual core of its people, it must a) find out at which of the three levels mentioned above its senior team is on; likewise for the management team and likewise for each level in the organisation; b) devise programmes commensurate with those levels ('When the student is ready, the teacher will appear' – so says an old Sufi proverb) and c) provide employees with mentoring over a period of time from spiritually developed mentors.

* * *

A second danger is that our current third-level business and management education system – in particular our MBA programmes – is not encouraging young people to understand themselves and the people they would manage from both an emotionally intelligent and spiritually intelligent point of view. The focus is still on IQ. The entry test to do an MBA, for example, is purely an IQ test. Neither emotional nor spiritual testing is required. The problems of tomorrow cannot be solved by the mindsets of today which created them. So we need to be building more EQ and even more importantly (because people are looking for greater depth than just the psychological 'pat on the head') more SQ taught in our Leadership and Management programmes. However, those talented in IQ only may completely discount SQ because, as Robert Quinn says, it is only 'as we conquer ourselves that we come in contact with a source of internal power that is not experienced by normal people living normalised lives.'[3]

* * *

A third danger: many organisations, whose backs are against the proverbial wall due to fiercely competitive conditions, manage the deep issues of their people – meaning, values, connection, for example – by separating them from other core functional areas, and even walling them off altogether, because they feel they need to put their energy into managing their 'core business' and spirituality is not seen by them as connected to that. Other organisations, not as financially pressed, simply do not see that spiritual matters have anything to do with daily work and bottom line and do not see the workplace as a setting to discuss the private concerns of employees. However, the fact of the matter is that these types of discussion do go on in organisations – at tea breaks, lunch breaks and on training programmes – and to ignore this is to create a 'psychological fragmentation and ambivalence'[4] in employees that can lead to depression. Depression accounts for over 100,000 lost man days per annum in Ireland alone and costs in excess of £290,000 million – £170,000 million of which is through lost time from work.[5]

*   *   *

A fourth danger that emerges is that at a time of enormous global upheaval (epitomised by the attacks on the World Trade Centre and the Pentagon in the US) it takes far more than values to sustain people. So, a focus on values alone will not be enough to create a spirituality intelligent organisation. Crises are the fast route to our spiritual core, because in an instant all the other ego props and cultural layers are taken away and we are forced to examine the deepest of levels within us. People with addictions such as narcotics, alcohol and food have known this for a long time. To overcome their addiction, they have had to reach into that deepest part of themselves to connect to their 'Higher Power' for a strength beyond the limitations of their own ability.

*   *   *

A fifth danger is the promulgation, by some consultants in the area of bringing spirituality into the workplace, that cultural change can be implemented in small companies in a matter of six to eight months. Deep change – as Robert Quinn calls it – takes time, a long time unless a crisis emerges to force people to re-evaluate their values and the base from which they live their lives. Some organisations have put their managers on lengthy self-discovery programmes such as those offered by the American Leadership Forum with the precise objective of helping spark that journey 'to the centre' within their managers. As I have mentioned before, some people are not prepared for the pain required to move into this core place. The reason for the pain is the psychological surgery required to remove the carbuncle software of the ego and culture states from the person. The ideal in terms of cultural change is to staff the organisation with people who are spiritually intelligent.

★   ★   ★

A sixth danger is the Law. In the US and Europe, legislation prevails to separate State from Church. Bringing spiritual intelligence into the workplace means being careful not to cross the legal line. Pacific Bell was legally challenged for spending millions on a training programme based in part on the teachings of an Armenian mystic; a Firestone Tyre manager in Georgia refused to conduct a training programme that conflicted with his own spiritual convictions.[6]

★   ★   ★

A seventh danger is that spiritual intelligence in the workplace programmes are set in a profit-dominated context and, therefore, *could be seen to be used* as tools to serve the prosperity of the company only. In business, profit – not love – is the key driver. However, if we look at spiritual intelligence as opposed to spirituality (which, as we have seen in Chapter Two, takes on a very broad meaning), it is impossible for the spiritually intelligent person, whose brain is experiencing 40Hz brain wave oscillations and temporal lobe (the God Spot in the brain) activity, to be manipulative or anything other than authentic.

★   ★   ★

An eighth danger: in the 'learning organisation', which we have seen is part of the spiritually aware organisation, employees are continuous learners. However, this puts them in a state of continuous learning deficit. Using the Myers-Briggs Temperament

Indicator[7] as a model to understand Temperament, those personalities that prefer closure (those who score a 'J' in MBTI) will be stressed by the lack of closure. Since this type comprises over 70% of the populace, that means a lot of stressed people.

* * *

A ninth danger results from the past experience of cult groups, which have bonded people with a vision, a purpose, a set of values and objectives, only to derail all of that by requiring the community to kill itself in a mass suicide. This brings up the thorny issue of evil, which our IQ and EQ environments find very difficult to tackle. It also highlights the need for a moral authority *beyond* the HR Director/CEO/Spiritual Mentor, i.e. the need for God, and this is where our atheists bow out. It is a difficult issue, but it nevertheless must be tackled, and if the *dialogue* process is used, then the sharing of ideas on this difficult issue will be much easier.

* * *

A tenth danger is that spirituality without the disciplines of prayer, meditation, fasting and worship (of God) is a vulnerable spirituality – vulnerable to the temptations of power, self and the cares of this world.

* * *

An eleventh danger focuses on the fact that spiritual intelligence (the temporal lobe activity and the 40hz brainwave oscillations) is purely connecting the individual to God and this, say mystics, is the only reason why we are here on this earth: to connect to God and have relationship with God. Spirituality, on the other hand, as seen in its various manifestations in the workplace, offers a cafeteria of options to fire up the true inner engine of the employee. However, that activity is not God-wards but towards the Company and, therefore, could be distracting people from the true 'eternal' reason for practising the many aspects of spirituality. Just as education has lost its role as true education and has become a preparation for the job market, so spiritual activity risks losing its true role in order to become a preparation for the survival of the twenty-first century organisation.

★ ★ ★

Notes

1. Matthew McKay and Patrick Fanning, *Self-Esteem* (Oakland, CA: New Harbinger Publications, 1991)

2. Richard Bandler, Steve Andreas (ed), Connirae Andreas (ed), *Using Your Brain – For a Change* (Real People, 1985)

3. Robert Quinn, *Change the World* (San Francisco: Jossey-Bass Inc., Pub., 2000), p. 22

4. Ian I. Mitroff and Elizabeth Denton, *A Spiritual Audit of Corporate America* (San Francisco, CA: Jossey-Bass Inc. Pub., 1999), p. 7

5. *Aware Magazine*, Summer 2000, Vol. 12, No. 2, p. 5

6. Tara Fenwick and Elizabeth Lange, 'The Turn To The Spiritual In Workplace Training and Development,' www.ualberta.ca/~tfenwick/ext/spirit.htm

7. David Keirsey and Marilyn Bates, *Please Understand Me* (Del Mar, CA: Prometheus Nemesis Books, 1978)

CHAPTER V

PERSONAL STORIES

We can be an inch deep
or one inch wide and a mile deep.
God wants us deeper in our faith and relationship with Him
and we should be concerned about how wide our influence is.
– Oliver Wendell Holmes

The Senior Executive

The journey has begun for many people through a defining event in their personal lives. So it was also with my journey. After three years of marriage my wife decided she had enough, and while I was on a business trip in Texas, USA, she left England with our two-year-old son for her family home in Ireland. The feelings of grief and loss that accompanies such a separation are unfortunately known by far too many people nowadays, and the process of recovery can be a long and tortuous route. Many people have great difficulty in recovering, and it is probably fair to say that almost all people who go through the trials of divorce and separation change to a very great extent.

In my case, however, the intervention came from God. It started simply. As I recounted my difficulties to a very good friend and colleague at the Texas plant, he asked me an inspired question – 'Do you know a Christian Councillor who could help?' The timing and phrasing of this question was crucial – I believe that no one in Europe would have asked the question in that manner, and that he too had a strong religious belief was also significant. The question lead me instantly to recall a person I had known from many years before, working in the field of personal development and training, but who also had a deep religious grounding and conviction. I rang that instant and with the patient advice I received I began a wonderful journey and development that has changed my life in a way no other event had changed it before. At this stage I can say that if I had not been in Texas, and had not heard exactly that sentence from my friend, I would never have made the crucial connection. God indeed works in mysterious ways from time to time, and ensures always that we are cared for in a very special way.

Moving forward

The advice I received was simple but very effective – 'you must know that God loves you and realise that you live in His love'. I began to say many (hundreds!) times a day the affirmations 'God loves me', 'God is Love' and 'Love loves me'. In this way I began my grounding in God's divine and unbounded love for us, His creation. In more recent times I have noted that when I 'forget' this most basic principle I am in danger of becoming 'unstuck' and this can lead to (temporary, thank God) losses of confidence and faith.

Because any development begins within, I began a programme of prayer, bible readings and commentary, with 'Thoughts for the day' type programmes from such books as *God Calling, Faith to Faith and My Utmost for His Highest*. In short I started putting God first – something I had never really done before.

The methods I used were simple – daily prayer, observance of the Sabbath, traditional practices and sacraments. In recent times I have begun to 'keep company with Jesus' more – imagining him sitting in the office and just talking to him about a problem we are having, or riding in the car together to work, or just sitting together in the house. This I find most real and very effective – in the turbulence of our modern lives, with television, radio, mobile phones and constant activity and inputs, it is so difficult, but conversely so important, to find some quiet time with the Lord.

Providing for my every need

As my journey progressed I discovered I was more and more able to hold an inner peace, and received many blessings from the Lord through prayer. In short, when I required something, I prayed for it in Jesus' name and my needs were fulfilled. Some of the answers and items received were indeed miraculous.

As I needed a cheaper house in which to live, but also a location of beauty and peace, I prayed and was granted a rented accommodation in the beautiful Devon countryside, just a short distance from work and the city and friends. To find such a treasure at a price I could afford was miraculous indeed, particularly given the local housing market!

There were many other blessings I received – too numerous to recall in these few lines – cheap flights to see my son when he was seriously ill, help in times of financial need, etc. All prayed for and received through the name of Jesus. I began to live in the love of God, relax in His presence, learn His word (from the Bible readings) and speak His word into every situation.

This is not to say I am by any means either holy or perfect. As it says in the book – 'why do you call me good. Only God is good.' It is just that before I was ashamed of my weakness, frightened to stand before God or go back to him after I had failed (again!). So I ran away, returning only when things got really bad or I wanted something – 'the giant vending machine in the sky – prayers in, miracles out'. But now I am beginning to realise that without him I am nothing, and it is only with His help and love that we can exist and succeed.

So by relaxing in His love, enjoying His companionship, speaking His words into the situation (especially when the sense evidence is contradictory) and by holding the mental picture I have seen some great happenings and changes in my life.

In the working environment
What I have found is that the same procedures work for our team in the factory. As a senior manager in a very large engineering business and being responsible for over 220 staff in a heavy manufacturing environment, one could assume that work would be pragmatic, logical and far removed from the spiritual realm? Nothing could be further from the truth!

God has blessed our efforts in the work environment also. He started by granting me advancement in my career in spite of my personal difficulties, allowing me to stay in England and not need to emigrate further overseas, as would otherwise have been the case. Through His grace my intensity level has decreased, making me easier to work with and for. He has also provided for us in many ways – achieving sales and shipping targets month after month through all types of impossible difficulties, in recent times limiting a £2 million plus quality problem to one of minor magnitude (£100k), and often we find that customers and suppliers co-operate with us at just the right instant to obtain the maximum positive effect – all through His word and our prayers.

Indeed it has come to pass that other managers and workers have passed comment on how calm and relaxed I am in my work and my workers accept the situation when I tell them that I need to pray about a particular problem or situation. From time to time I have also been bold enough to state what the outcome will be having prayed about it – going with the feeling that came through the grace of God. Thank God these outcomes have always come to pass as stated through His glory and majesty.

This is not to say that we have thrown away all the tools and techniques often described as best practice and now make products through faith alone! No, by overlaying the spiritual principles outlined above we are now more effective, more loved and more successful than ever before. As our confidence and faith increases I am sure that the Lord will work even more wonders in our workplace.

All praise and thanksgiving and honour and glory be given to God the Almighty Father now and forever.

Moving forward in faith and love
A key part of my development has been the continual realisation that God loves me and accepts me imperfect though I am. He continues to overlook my faults and failings, while all the time gently calling me to Him, and encouraging me to do better. In many ways I find that He treats me exactly as we do a small child ('The kingdom of Heaven belongs to such as these') – forgiving them the persistent messes they create, wiping up afterwards and encouraging me to do better in a kind and gentle way. It is a real process of continual improvement – a little at a time every day.

In previous times I was ashamed of the times I made mistakes and went wrong, and hid from God in pride and arrogance. Now I know that this is exactly the wrong thing to do – when things go wrong and we have committed sin that is the time we need God most, that is the time we need His love and forgiveness – to run away from Him then is playing right into the hands of Satan!

Prayer
In order to preserve any friendship we need to stay in touch. I find that now I want to spend some time every day with Jesus,

who is my friend and Lord, and talk to God the Father who is also my Father. The basis of this is, of course, love. If I love God and He loves me then it is most natural that we would wish to spend some time together every day. This can be done in many ways – praying, meditating, or just going for a walk together – knowing that He is present in all things and at all occasions! This relaxation in His love and presence is very fulfilling and very rewarding. I feel whole even though I am alone. I do not feel any fear, any disturbance, any depression. ('Even though I walk in the valley of the shadow of death no evil will I fear, You are there…'.)

It is also good to listen to God, who knows all things and gives the most perfect of advice. I find I best do this through reading the Bible – His word – and drawing little lessons from it. The usual way to describe this is to 'meditate' on His word – personally I am not the greatest at 'meditation', so this 'meditation on the word' always seems to put me off. For me I find it best to read a short commentary in one of the many books available (*Faith to Faith, My Utmost for His Highest*, etc.) and before or after reading the word. Also a good daily prayer web site can be found at http://www.jesuit.ie/prayer/index.htm – this is really good and the process used is very helpful.

I also find that 'praise stilleth the enemy', and therefore I find that reading the Psalms out loud helps a lot. It is of course possible to choose a Psalm that suits the occasion or mood – Psalms of praise, forgiveness, peace, joy, etc. It is also good to remember that not only was David a great champion and King, but also a poet and musician and many of his verses are particularly powerful.

The community of Christ
As a Catholic by tradition the Mass has always been something of a weekly event for me. At first because I was expected to go – the usual weight of expectation from family and community. Then in my early twenties I stopped going for a while, but later

found that I wanted to go, as if there was something missing from my week if I did not. I expect that some of this is traditional or a throwback to my upbringing, but I believe something deeper lies behind it – we all need a sense of community and sharing, a ritual or tradition that keeps up together and grounded in belief. A very unusual allegory may be a sports team – it is important as a member of a sports team to show up to the practice session once a week – that through the session we gain a feeling of togetherness, a feeling of team spirit and oneness. Often on more serious teams, coaches will suggest that injured players also show up to the sessions, even of they can't fully participate in the activities – just to be there, to show their faces and to encourage others through their commitment to the team and presence. They in turn tend to feel less of the isolation that is so often felt by athletes when recovering from injury – their team-mates wish them well for a speedy recovery.

It is the same with Mass. Through our presence we give others a little lift just by being there – we see that we are not alone in our humanity before God, even though we may not know of their joys or sorrows. Also God sees us there, even if our attention lapses, or we are distracted, He appreciates our efforts to take some time out to be with Him and His community. We also get the benefit of joining the community in receiving our Lord in the Eucharist as well as the spiritual gifts present in the occasion.

Hence dwelling in love, praising and worshipping the Lord our God, spending time in His presence and finding Him in the world around me daily, helps me develop in belief and closeness to God. Through prayer and study of His word I learn how to implement His will in my life, and receive strength and courage when difficulties arise. By weekly attendance at Mass I feel a togetherness that is so very human and often so very necessary. It is also through these actions that I grow in love of God, with all the great things this entails.

The Company Director

I have always 'believed' in the existence of God, but He played no direct, tangible part in my daily life. He was just out there somewhere and, like many people, I turned to Him in times of crises, etc., but without any deep or true understanding of, or commitment to, Him.

I have lived a safe, happy life, by many standards. Always having the support of family and friends, and have had no major crises or hardships to endure. I went through a marriage separation and a long-term relationship break-up, with difficulties, but I survived and just muddled through somehow.

Over a fifteen-year period I worked to build up a small but profitable business in Dublin City. Looking back, this was my area of greatest difficulty, and it was through this situation that God was introduced into my life, which has now changed dramatically and forever.

With hindsight, and many sessions of counselling, I now understand that my main problem and unhappiness was caused by the diametrically opposing personalities of my business partner and myself, and the fact that God played no part in our business or personal lives.

We could not have been more different and had no skills to deal with these differences – which were good for the balanced development of the business, but for us on a personal level they were disastrous. One day in 1998 in sheer desperation – a point I had often been at before – I asked a friend to recommend someone in the H. R. area who could advise us. The only option I could see was to break up the partnership. This would have been a very painful experience for both of us and also a great waste of many years' hard work and commitment, on both our parts.

I have absolutely no doubt that his recommendation was God-directed. In spite of a very busy schedule our 'mentor' was free to see us within days. At a brief initial meeting our 'mentor', amazingly, saw our personality differences and difficulties. We started working with her immediately and while we had to address many issues which were very painful and unpleasant for us both, we stuck with it and I believe that we have now both changed our approach to, and understanding of, one another and others.

From the very beginning, our 'mentor' introduced the concept of 'love' and talked openly to us about God and Jesus and having Him in our personal and work environments. This was not at all what I had expected and, to be honest, I found it uncomfortable, to say the least. But we both knew that this was probably our last chance and so we took on board her (difficult) exercises and suggestions.

Three years later we are still working together and we have developed the business into new and interesting areas. Our personalities have not changed, but we have learned how to handle our differences and to work together in love and harmony. It was not an easy road and many times I felt like just walking away from it all. We still have a way to go but with God's amazing grace and presence in our lives I believe that we will make it.

For the past year we have had daily readings from spiritual books in the office, and can now pray together and talk to God about what we need and want for the day. Again, this practice was very strange and even uncomfortable for me, but it has now become a way of life and part of our daily office routine. This new spirituality in the office has changed the 'feel' of the business and the working environment.

On a personal note, God is now so much part of my life that I cannot get out of bed in the mornings without talking to Him, thanking Him for so many good things in my life, but most importantly, asking Him/His Spirit to be with me in everything that I do during the day.

I try to be aware of Him in all that I do, and stop and focus on Him before making, say, an important phone call. I even ask Him to provide a parking space outside the office for me if I am under pressure! And He always does! On the other hand, on days when I am not in a rush, I tell Him 'It's OK. I don't need the space today.' This personal chit-chat with God is now a permanent feature of my life. I don't think I could live any other way now and hope that I never will.

Marketing Consultant/Human Potential Consultant/Writer

'A small boy of determined spirits fired by an unquenchable faith in his mission can alter the course of history'
– Gandhi

For many years now I have been searching for the secret to a more fulfilled, happier existence. At each stage on this ongoing journey I was convinced I had it, only to discover that my thinking was flawed, something was missing. When I discovered the latest answer, and chose to integrate it into my life, the magic truly began. Initially let me take you through some of the trip.

In 1966 I was born into a middle-class family in a small town in Roscommon, Ireland. My father and mother shared responsibility for running the family business, a petrol station and convenience store. In addition, my father worked as a Community Welfare Officer five days a week. While he worked my mother ran the business, simultaneously looking after the five young ones! Time off was a rare luxury for my parents as the family business closed for four days in the year.

In 1987 I left college, individualistic at a superficial level and destined to take my rightful place with the 'majority'. My first significant stop was to subscribe to the success movement. This would be the key to a happier existence, I reasoned. Success, as defined by the Concise Oxford Dictionary is the 'attainment of wealth, fame, or position'. The majority at that time, the yuppie generation, ate, slept and drank money. Becoming part of, as Nietzche describes it, 'the damned compact majority', was a more comfortable, yet unfulfilling choice. I, the young initiate at the age of twenty-four, pursued all of its trappings with vigour.

Between 1987 and 1990, after weaving my marketing magic in three companies, one in Ireland and two in the UK, I had enough money to pursue my desires in cosmopolitan London.

In late 1990 I returned to Ireland and established Advanced Marketing. Consistent in purpose, the 'conditioned' target was to accumulate wealth. The strategy was simple, I had to work harder if I wanted to control my destiny. Success was ninety-nine percent perspiration, one percent inspiration, or so they said. The paradigm was about control. Lenin was right: 'freedom is good, but control is better'.

By 1995 my 'mission' was accomplished, my earnings had exceeded my wildest dreams, yet I felt uncomfortable – unfulfilled. Financial empowerment was no remedy for this feeling. Certainly something was missing. My relationship with my girlfriend wasn't filling the void either. Success it seems does not come gift-wrapped in happiness. It was obviously time for me to change the paradigm, time to look for new answers.

In search of answers, I travelled extensively – India, Peru, Australia, USA, Israel and Europe. Each trip seemed to happen at the right time, every time, helping to deepen my distinctions. Each was the catalyst for growth.

In 1996 while attending a course in the US, I was intuitively drawn to seek guidance from a stranger. Anton, a German, was the ex-CEO of a multinational company. He warned me that I was likely on my current life curve to ascend to the top quickly only to find there were no other mountains to climb. A personal crisis, he predicted, would ensue. His advice was simple. Take some time out to contemplate, to let my internal wisdom dictate my course. This was my first wake-up call. A time-out to my rational mind up to this was the ultimate waste of time! Two years later an astute, happy, centred Indian reconfirmed the importance of his message. 'You need not have left my house,' he declared, 'the secret is within.' The more time spent in silence and contemplation, the more my inner whispers were providing me with much guidance.

A few months after going to India I travelled to Tibet. One night I awoke with an abundance of energy rushing through my veins. I rushed over to my backpack, pulled out my writing pad and starting scribbling furiously. Whatever came to mind was noted. First up: the secrets to prolonged periods of happiness in your life – an awkward headline I thought, but, accepting that every emotion comes and goes, it was accurate. We can't be happy all the time, but we can be happier more of the time.

> Step one: identify the unique talent you possess.
> Step two: use it for the good of all human beings.
> Step three: trust.

The process, I sensed, must be underpinned by principles, by natural laws of integrity, honesty, trust, love, etc. Thus there are three critical elements for finding and living your mission: identify, serve, and trust. Serving from the centre was all-important. I remembered the words of the Chinese Proverb, 'The right means in the hands of the wrong person will always turn out badly'. The wise person shares his/her wisdom, just like every great teacher I met on my journey. That night, I committed to identifying my mission.

After reviewing the highs and lows in life, my purpose had become crystal clear – to inspire, motivate and assist people in making the right choices in life, not just in Ireland but right around the world. It is important to note that entering the dark is part of the journey and should help further define your mission. By exploring the dark and light we can gain a deeper understanding of what our mission is. 'Your pain is the breaking of the shell that encloses your understanding' – Kahlil Gibran.

When I released my mission to the universe, the magic truly began. Release and detach, let go and let God – that was, and still is, my strategy. One that has opened up doors in all aspects of my life, from the teachers I attracted, to new friends, to finding my soulmate, to attracting the biggest deal of my life. When our mission is released to the universe the details are taken care of as if by some invisible force; by the Universal Source, for me – by God. Let me review the fairytale which ensued after releasing and detaching:

Letting go: the book
In 1997, it was time to extend my personal boundaries, venture outside my comfort zone yet again. The goal was to write a personal excellence book of my own – a best-seller – and in the process positively touch peoples lives around the country. I released my intention to the universe. A few technical problems existed. Firstly, my command of written English wasn't impressive, having just scraped a pass in my school exams. Moreover as yet, life's full picture hadn't yet emerged, I needed more teachers – I had much to learn. My old paradigm would have suggested knocking down the doors of potential teachers. My current belief system allowed me to detach and wait.... I let go and let God. I consoled myself by contemplating on the old axiom, 'When the student is ready, the teacher appears'. Well, as expected, they did appear. Within a few months teachers from around the globe – Irish, Australians, Americans and English – arrived to help me on my journey. Even closer to home I was to meet a wonderful teacher who would help me very much on my new path in life. On a Tuesday afternoon, a knock came to my door – a lady with whom I had exchanged only pleasantries had heard of my plans to write a book. She herself was a writer and in the past a teacher. Yes, I thought, the universe works perfectly. My new friends constructively dissected my manuscript, offering much needed direction and inspiration. Months later the book had motivated many people

to stray outside their comfort zones, to live life to the fullest. Over 11,000 copies of *How? When you don't know how* have been sold in Ireland. It has even been adopted by the education sector.

Letting go: finding a soulmate
I met my soulmate the day before my scheduled departure for the USA. We 'clicked' almost immediately. In the middle of the night she went missing. For one of the few times in my life I started playing the 'poor me' tape. Typical, just when you think your 'search' is over a new one begins! I found Deirdre upstairs in my friend's house. She had just put my friend's child to bed and was staying with her until she fell asleep. Knowing that this was her first time in the house, I was more than touched by her compassionate and caring disposition. One big problem, I was off to the US in the morning. Regardless, that night, I asked her to join me in the US. In my 34 years on the planet, I for whatever reasons wasn't willing to commit. Now in what seemed like no more than 34 minutes, I was ready. I knew it was right. What next?

Let go and trust. I had to stick to a winning life strategy. In the following three months our only means of communication was by phone. As the days passed we shared stories from our past. On one such occasion Deirdre told me that she had appeared on TV twice as an Irish dancer. At that time I was looking for an Irish dancer for my corporate training program! Coincidence? No. Another by-product of trust. On 25 September, I returned for a brief visit to Ireland. We met at the airport. To the rational mind – our second date. To us, the start of our life together. It was everything I had dreamed of and more. The sick feeling I experienced at the baggage claim in addition to the negative thoughts that engulfed my mind on and off were all history within moments of our rendez-vous. Three months later, she joined me in California. We worked together on our first major speaking engagement. And as they say in fairytales – which do happen – we lived happily ever after! We are now both living in San Francisco. On 31 July 2001 we got engaged in Hawaii. The relationship has, in my opinion, vindicated my belief that we should hold out for the fairytale relationship. This assertion elicited much controversy in my homeland when *How? When you don't know how* was published. A fairytale doesn't have to be a myth; it can be our reality.

Letting go: business

Five months after launching my book, I took the leap of faith – I honoured my uncomfortable feeling and my new found buzz. With trust in my heart I formed a new business, 'Kevin Kelly Unlimited', focused completely on adding value to peoples lives. Implementation was going to be problematic. To truly follow my mission involved kicking to touch six years of blood, sweat and tears. It involved leaving the old culturally embraced paradigm behind by shedding ninety per cent of my income. My rational colleagues found my decisions bizarre to put it mildly. All work from 'my past lives' was graciously refused. But there was even more upheaval to come. While in Israel in 1999, my inner whispers were pushing me to move to the USA. With trust in my heart, I committed to the move. Progress was slow but sure. After a few months I decided to take a holiday; I needed a break. Dream ticket. On my return flight from Ireland I sat beside a very pleasant lady who engaged me in conversation. We spoke for most of the time for our short flight to London. Halfway through the conversation she committed herself to opening up the market for me. A week later, as promised, she booked me for a very important engagement with her trainers. This appointment opened up the whole market for my training package. It was also the most lucrative assignment in my career to date. 'Coincidentally', I was trying to get back to America for the previous three days.

Letting go: research

As mentioned earlier, I have travelled extensively. My only compass/map/plan was to trust and to see what happened. In November 1999 I travelled to Israel. On the plane, just after the movie *Notting Hill* had finished, nature called. I needed to go to the toilet as a matter of urgency. One problem, the passenger on my right side was blocking my way and he was asleep. Not wanting to disturb his siesta time, I struggled with nature for another few minutes. Finally, I had no choice… well actually I had, but this was not a desirable option! 'Sorry,' I gently shrieked, 'Can I get by you, I must go to the bathroom.' He politely moved aside. Nature had obviously called other people on the plane also, as a queue had developed. Honouring my friendly Irish disposition, I engaged the girl in front of me in conversation. She was going to work in Jerusalem for a few days. A taxi was waiting at the airport to collect her. In contrast, my thoughts were to go to Tel Aviv, take a few days to get my bearings, then later on in the week travel to Jerusalem asap and station myself there. The more I spoke to her, the more I knew that a direct route to Jerusalem would be the most appropriate choice. Something inside of me was promoting this choice – a knowing without the knowledge. This is what I choose to do, in the interesting company of the 'Belfast girl'.

The staff at the hotel were excellent, Bassam the Manager was articulate and informative. I explained my position to him. My objective was to interview people whose stories could teach and inspire others. The more angles to the story the better. He committed himself to the cause. It wasn't long before he delivered. That afternoon, after making a few phone-calls, he asked me: 'Would you like to interview one of the leaders of the Palestinian Prisoners who has just been released?' This could be organised after consulting with his friend.'Yes,' I exclaimed, excitement oozing out of every atom in my body. The thought of interviewing a 'terrorist' or 'freedom fighter' pushed adrenaline through my cells. Jamhil was a huge interview to get in Israel at that time. Now, if I had gone to the toilet one minute earlier...! The above is merely a snapshot of the life I have been blessed to live. I have no doubt that trust is the definitive life strategy.

I have learned to live my mission, to do it with love, so that it will truly be a legacy worth leaving.

The Bank Manager

My job was taking a toll on my life – there never seemed to be enough time, I didn't feel a sense of achievement, I worried a lot about how effective I was, what was I adding each day in my job. I felt disorganised, unfulfilled and unhappy. The unhappiness and despair I felt impacted on the other elements of my life – my time with my family, my friends and my marriage. I was not good company either in work or outside. The downward spiral had a ripple effect and I was losing confidence in my ability to enjoy and savour each day and in terms of work, even though all around me was the positive evidence of my achievements. I was in too negative a state of mind to notice. Something was wrong. I had lost my way and I went in search of finding my true sense, my true purpose. I wanted to be calm and peaceful and to greet each day as a gift. I had always believed in something greater, I had been brought up a Catholic but I didn't really practice, as I felt the Church was so removed from my world. Yet I always had faith and believed in God, or a universal force, which was good – but how could I make this real and apply it realistically to my day to day life / work.

It started very simply – a conscious decision to ask God to be a part of my life. I had a simple conversation with him and I asked him to come into my life, to guide me in all things and to show me how to develop my relationship with him. It felt like a new romance, little by little I discovered the nature of this wonderful father – I excitedly searched and read material that would tell me more about his nature and how I could get to know him better. The most important thing I learned was how much he loved me. With such a wonderful source of love I felt things beginning to change, it is hard to describe, it is so magical. The more you read/learn about your spirit (your connection and relationship with God), the more you want to know. Everything changes, your whole perspective on things and situations

I could see the evidence of my new relationship with God impacting my whole life – when you bring love into every situation, no matter how difficult, there can be no fear and it is amazing the things that can happen. Let me share some of the practical benefits I have experienced in my work and life:

- my whole view of fear is different. I recognise it and can use the word of God to remove it from my heart and mind. This allows me to approach each problem/issue/person/ circumstance with an openness and willingness. This has lead to increased trust and wonderful relationships – the benefits in terms of teamwork and productivity has been tremendous;
- I worry less and I am calmer and more peaceful. I hand over difficult situations to God. I pray that He intervenes and ask for his help. I am more relaxed and free to be myself;
- I have more energy to carry out my duties, and enthusiasm to beat the band. The joy I feel each day I pass to my work colleagues, and the atmosphere at work is great;
- I see all situations/circumstances that confront me as something sent by God for me to learn from. It's amazing how this attitude can change situations;
- my presence has grown, I am stronger, and the feedback I have received from work colleagues has been wonderful;
- my interests have expanded – each day is truly a gift and I have much to contribute and much to praise and thank God for.

God is now the source of my every need, each day I take time to ensure I have spent quality time just being with Him. This takes several forms:

- reading His word, understanding it and applying it to my life;
- time with nature, enjoying his wonderful creation;
- time in silence just knowing his nature;
- time praising and thanking him for the wonderful blessings He bestows on me each moment;
- time in service – whatever work I am doing I do well, knowing I am serving Him;
- I see God in everyone and everything, and treat everyone and everything with dignity and love.

I am happy and in control of my life. I have peace in my heart and I know with such wondrous love as my source I can cope with whatever the world throws at me. Everyday I take time to serve him but more importantly I take time to be with him

The Human Resource Director

'What if you are wrong?' An innocent enough question put to me by a friend and colleague. This question in reality became a very complex one. Up to that time, about five years ago, I was neither a believer nor a disbeliever, I had ceased to think about life or its meaning.

My earlier upbringing was Catholic, and at the tender age of seventeen I entered the 'exciting world of work', full of ambition, ideas, motivation and the joys of teenhood.

Many myths were shattered by this early experience, I found hatred, spite, drunkenness and many excesses, including what is now termed as bullying. I left my surreal world of ideas and dreams and had to deal with the 'real world'. I became quite ruthless, idealistic and later in my career confident to a level bordering on arrogance. These combined to trigger my adrenalin and fan the flames of my ego. Statements like 'you are very opinionated' and 'nakedly ambitious' were levelled at me.

Back to the question. At this time I was a senior manager with a large global organisation and about to undergo a series of events that would change my life forever, my *modus operandi*, my outlook, my values, my raison d'être.

'Friends' conspired to plot my downfall – who needs an enemy with friends like these. These pseudo-friends, all of whom I had saved from the daggers of destruction at one time or another, traduced and libelled me. My integrity as a person and as a professional was attacked in a very malicious way. This resulted in a period of unprecedented trauma and stress for me, my family and close friends. This trauma and stress was compounded by my completing a major course of study.

Enter my friend and colleague, she who had asked the question what if you are wrong. I deliberated on this and other questions for some time and thought if I'm wrong on this substantive issue then I may well be wrong on other issues as well. If that was the case then I would be in serious trouble on a number of fronts. I deliberated on the meaning of life, the miracle of birth, the mystery of death and life's continuum.

These deliberations led me to meditation, communing with nature, being non-judgemental, supportive, 'tuning in to the cosmos', spirituality and seeking ways to help.

A new and different world was opening up. We inverted some popularly held notions and came up with 'it's the early worm that gets caught' and 'worms are at the top of the food chain'. From here to others: 'How many apples in a seed?' and 'How many ideas in a jar?'. One question (there are many) still unanswered is 'How does the moon have any affect on the earth's tides when at 150 plus miles up we have zero gravity and the moon is 250,000 miles distant with a land mass a fraction of the earth?' More to be had from quantum physics.

During my 'shafting' process some real friends and associates rallied round me. They, with my family and a legal colleague, helped me through the insanity that was going on. One of these colleagues, a close friend, deeply religious, exuding unconditional love, offered many insights into the worlds of quantum physics and spirituality. Over and over the words from the bible echoed 'What you ask the father for in my name will be given to you'. My most often used request now is 'In the name of Jesus I ask the Father for....'

The end of my career with that organisation came amid utter confusion, doubt and panic. At times death would have been a welcome relief from the mental anguish. This state lasted for many months. Family, friends and an old friend, Jesus, helped deal with endings and new beginnings. These beginnings were exciting. I was now free, tuning in, communing with nature and practising unconditionality. Free to be totally creative, innovative and helpful in a much more meaningful way, still ambitious but in a different way, an achieving and supportive way. Achievement based on competence; no false dreams or journeys into 'surrealism'.

What then were the key influences? Several friends and colleagues, some close friends, my special friend Jesus and very importantly my family who made many sacrifices. My changes resulted from the journeys I embarked upon. My experiences and I drew heavily on many books, some of which I will mention: *Seven Spiritual Laws of Success* by Deepak Chopra, *Awareness* by Antony De Mello, *In The Spirit of Business* by Robert Rosskind, *The Intuitive Manager* by Roy Rowan, *Brain Sex* by Ann Moir and David Jessels and various short extracts from the world of quantum physics, spirituality and mind-body healing.

From these readings two phrases stand out, one already mentioned, 'If you ask the Father anything in my name it will be given to you', and 'Inherent in every desire is the mechanism for its fulfilment'.

Now almost six years later on my new journeys, my greatest journey was to me. I travelled inwards to the depths of my being, to the core of my mind, now hoping to influence events mentally as well as physically by believing in and practising the two phrases in the previous paragraph.

Yes the industrial world is at times very stressful and a brutal place to be, with no love lost between the warring factions, using up valuable energy and resources in political dog-fighting in the name of business progress and profit. In this cauldron, spirituality must find a place to flourish and blossom. People will be attracted to those companies which espouse optimisation rather than maximisation, organisations which have a balance between business and demonstrated values.

I look forward to the next half century of challenges, feeling honoured to be asked to assist individuals and organisations achieve their potential, tutoring young entrepeneurs and intrepeneurs, future business leaders.

My journeys will continue, often in controversy, often in a minority of one, in a state of connectedness, full of optimism and now exuding unconditional love. I sank to the depths of despair, but with the help of friends, family and Jesus I came through the tunnel, I saw the light, I now bask in the light, multiple rainbows beckoning, abundance there for the asking. Greed is the antithesis of abundance and shortages caused by marketeers in pursuit of profit maximisation. Nature in its own way has provided all we will ever need. All we have to do is discover where the solutions are; the supply is infinite.

Take these two examples of abundance to illustrate the point: the common dandelion possesses a phenomenal amount of life chemicals, yet all we do is dig them up and let them die; gold, an international measure of wealth and affluence, is stockpiled in various vaults, converted to jewellery and with some still in the ground, no more or less since time began.

Real wealth comes from sharing, unconditional love, giving, receiving, helping, believing, doing.

As yet I do not profess to be religious, I may never do. How then do I describe myself in the context of all of the aforementioned? A visionary, a futurist, full of awareness, a 'spiritual' Christian. The world is now a much more beautiful place to be. I have awakened.

The IT Consultant

I recently moved from a large IT Services company because of my disillusionment with the internal culture and service focus of the organisation. The organisation was spending too much time and energy in providing for its own existence, consuming the skills and resources of the employees for no customer benefit.

Employees were immersed in a political and administrative mire, resulting in loss of focus on the customer, and therefore diminishing the value individuals perceived in themselves. 'Share Options' and 'Bonus Payments' were used to maintain the status quo, and were not based on 'real' added value. These incentives were only a further indication of the organisation's attempt to perpetuate itself, rather then rise to the challenge of providing its customers with service excellence, and its employees with a sense of personal value.

The organisation had a very limited view of the value created by the employee/customer and employee/employee relationships, which actually provided the organisation with a large part of its goodwill. In a lot of cases, customers were employee's customers, with limited loyalty to the organisation. I very much feel that the future in this industry will involve groups of skilled individuals coming together to provide particular customer services, whether on a continuous or on a once-off basis. These individuals will trade in their skills, maximising the energy available for customer service and 'life-style' choices.

In our modern, educated society, the individual's search for meaning, the desire to be part of something with a purpose, is best fulfilled by individuals taking control of themselves as a resource, to work as they wish with others in the search for this meaning, utilising all of the innate skills at their disposal.

The Interior Designer

Growing up as a 'middle' child, I was very shy, lacked confidence in my own abilities and felt very dependant on others for any success that I may perhaps, one day, achieve, if that could ever be possible. I have two amazing sisters and an older brother and we are very close as well as being best friends. I always felt, however, that I was very insignificant compared to them. My older brother and sister were always great communicators and my younger sister was very funny, the comic of the family, and then there was me, boring, old dull me. Of course, all this was my perception of things – I didn't ever realise until I was older that my brother and sisters had their own internal struggles.

Our family didn't have a lot of money and I developed a belief that money, fine things and travelling to exotic places would bring me the happiness I was looking for. Well, I married at a young age to escape my struggles and with my husband, who worked for one of the major international oil companies, travelled around the world for several years. We had lots of money, experienced lots of different good things and were very comfortable, but the inner peace for me was still not there. I then felt that to bring fulfilment we needed to start a family, and when I discovered I was pregnant, I was very excited. However, with the arrival of my beautiful son, I realised that although I was aware of this incredible gift, instead of being fulfilled, I was having to give, to this very needy little person, all of myself and, still being so broken inside, this magnified my feelings of inadequacy and low self confidence. I felt like a useless mother and a complete failure. On top of this, my husband, just six weeks after the birth of our baby, was travelling again with his work and I spent almost the first year of our son's life on my own. This was not the family life I had envisaged.

Half way through my son's first year, however, God stepped in, or should I say, made me realise that He was always with me. I had grown up in a very religious home but had never really known God as Father, Jesus as Saviour or the Holy Spirit as Comforter and Friend. My younger sister by this time had come into a personal relationship with God and was very excited about her life. It sounded ridiculous to me – her letters were full of God this and God that and I love God and He makes me feel amazing, etc., etc., and to me it sounded like a 'cult' fad. At the time, she was staying on a little island called Papa Stour in the Shetlands and she invited my husband and myself and our little son to come and visit. Nothing could have been further from my mind, however, than what faced me when we arrived.

When my husband and I arrived on Papa Stour, I was immediately met with the strongest presence I have ever experienced of good and evil. The presence of evil was very disturbing, but the presence of good was all encompassing and gave me incredible peace. It reached right into my heart and as a result I couldn't stop thinking about God and who He was and what He wanted from me. I learned later that this tiny little island was split into two groups, those who worshiped God and those involved with the occult. I left the island desperately wanting to know more about God and feeling very vulnerable apart from Him – I didn't realise at that time that He was, by His amazing love, grace and mercy, drawing me to Him. My older sister, who had also been to the island and who also experienced the Love and Presence of God whilst there, came to visit me and at that time, after prayer and discussions, I surrendered my life to Jesus and asked Him to step into my life and live His Life in and through me. For the first time in my life, I experienced peace and joy in my heart and for me, more importantly, acceptance and value, and all this within myself –

not trying to attain this from externals such as things or places or being busy or whatever, but from within, where God lives.

I learned that, as with all relationships, constant contact keeps everything alive and God loves to 'chat' with his family, so prayer is very important and not prayer as in a formal kind of prayer (although that certainly has its place too and is very appropriate on occasions) but prayer as in talking to God and bringing issues to Him. Also reading and meditating on His Word is very important to me. God's Word is who He is and I believe we all need to know who He is to be like Him. God speaks through His Word. In my personal studies I ask the Holy Spirit to direct me to where He wants me to read from in the Word and, often its just a very few verses of scripture, but God does a lot of talking through those words.

Now with a family of three grown boys and working in a very busy design practice, more than ever I value the wisdom that God gives me. Being a Christian woman in the workplace often means that I go the extra mile and I always ensure that I give my best and I am aware that, because of these attitudes, my colleagues rely on me and, in turn, my responsibility in the business has grown considerably. God tells us that we really work for Him and that whether our employer sees what we do or not shouldn't stop us from giving our best at all times. In the past, I could never have even considered doing the work I do: I would have been afraid of the limelight, the responsibility, the very thought of having to bring in business and the demands of maintaining and strengthening the existing client base. Now, I just have my 'board meetings' with God, lay out before Him what aspects of the business need His help, and leave it in His hands, expecting to receive the answers from my loving Heavenly Father. And they always come. So, in terms of the business, I can be at peace and use my energy to create rather than to be fearful and anxious.

In times past, I would have been very withdrawn, lacking confidence in my abilities and unable to communicate effectively with other people. I didn't realise at the time that how we perceive ourselves is transmitted to others and, sadly, because I did not see my own worth, neither did anyone else and I found myself often overlooked or bypassed, not only in the workplace but in my own personal life too. I found dealing with people on a one-to-one basis very difficult. I couldn't see that the person I would be dealing with would of course only be discussing a business matter with me, instead, I felt that they were examining me and criticising me and then ultimately deciding that I wouldn't be 'up for the job'. Because I am now aware of 'who I am', I love having the opportunity of one-to-one meetings and I know that not only am I well able to provide an excellent service to our clients and business associates but I am also a good team player within our Practice, i.e. providing an excellent support to my colleagues where possible – even with personal issues. I now know that God has made me who I am and has given me the personality I have and that these 'qualities' are very important. I have learned to value myself and my contribution and I know that others, too, value what I have to say. What a change from the timid little girl of yesterday.

The Chief Executive
James Lovelock's *GAIA: A new way of looking at life* was perhaps the spur to my search for a better way of being. Lovelock, an eminent atmospheric scientist, during the early 1960s formulated a model that is perhaps the most surprising and most beautiful expression of self-organisation – the idea that the planet Earth as a whole is a living, self-organising system.

Lovelock commented on the effect his book had on his neighbours in West Cork, Ireland, where he lived at that time, an effect that astonished him. The effect on these people was of a spiritual rather than an intellectual nature. The GAIA hypothesis had and continues to have a similar effect on myself. But why the personal search for a better way of being? As a younger man, my energies were extremely focussed and directed. The focus and direction, however, were on things rather than on being, on the material rather than the spiritual. Consequently, the desired outcomes of many actions taken by me were that I would conquer whatever challenge or problem presented itself. The challenges over time became more and more to do with work rather than with myself or with my family. 'Driven' was a word often associated with me – 'the man who works hard and plays hard' being a compliment. Many hours were spent at work in the pursuit of some challenge, real or perceived. Work hours would be followed by a similarly intense involvement with an amateur drama society, directing people and things; or with a local sports team, again directing. Being in control of people and events was the ultimate satisfaction – or was it? Perhaps not, for the completion of one event ensured a more intense involvement in the next one and the one after that and so on.

When my marital separation came it was a complete shock. Being so busy with everything else, I had ignored all the signs warning me of my apparent lack of interest in the family. 'How could this be,' I thought, 'having worked myself to the bone to ensure that the family wanted for nothing; a nice house, good schools and education' – the unfairness of it all! On Friday evening – everything; Sunday evening – nothing! Bitterness abounded!

The disintegration of my life's pattern coincided with a change of job and a consequent geographical relocation. For the next couple of years I immersed myself in work; 70-hour working weeks became the norm. I became obsessed with the technicalities of organising and reorganising the company. People were treated as parts of the company and some became extremely stressed as a result of pressure from me to change rapidly. The changes perceived as necessary by me did take place and a new company management structure emerged, leading to a more efficient organisation.

Nevertheless, the feeling of unease, of ultimate non-fulfilment, within me, still persisted.

Robert E. Lane, author of *The Loss of happiness in Market Democracies* (1996), contends that, whilst citizens of advanced market democracies are satisfied with their material progress, a spirit of unhappiness often haunts many. He shows that the main sources of well-being in advanced economies are friendships and a good family life. Conversely, as prosperity increases, there is a tragic erosion of family solidarity and community integration, leading to individuals becoming more distrustful of one another and their political institutions. I can relate to this hypothesis.

The change came about imperceptibly, though subtly enabled, I later realised, by a couple of people whose influence was directed at the spiritual rather than the physical aspects of my own life. Rather than concentrate on the organisational outcomes of the change processes, it gradually dawned upon me that the focus of endeavour should be directed towards the fulfilment of the individual needs of the employee in terms of their work and, by extension, their lives. The change within me, therefore, was away from a mechanistic, Newtonian, worldview towards a holistic, ecological view.

The outcomes of this change within myself were reflected in an organisational imperative that put the individual first. Putting the needs of the individual first, it was found, ensured that the desired outcomes are achieved more readily than when only the outcomes themselves are concentrated upon.

The organisation, once driven and outcome focused, is now recognised by its commitment to the development of its entire people: staff, customers, managers and other stakeholder groups. Individual and group excellence is encouraged and expected; respect for the individual is an absolute requirement of all participants in the organisation; training and personal development is offered on an ongoing basis; family-friendly work practices are the norm; an employee assistance programme is in place and widely availed of.

This change in emphasis from the business to the individual and from the mechanistic to the holistic has had a most pleasing result. In the year 2000, following an intensive review by an international management consultancy group, the organisation was credited with having achieved a level of managerial competencies and organisational climate far superior to that normally achieved by similar organisations throughout Europe. The effect on employees of this review has been one of singular satisfaction accompanied by renewed confidence in themselves and their organisation. The effects on the users of the service provided by the organisation are almost exponential in extent, with service users now being the recipients of the individual attention resulting in increased competencies and skills.

But what of the writer? Well, the exploration continues by way of an ongoing communion with the surrounding universe. The questions become more profound but the journey towards fulfilment no less demanding. The daily living, however, is so much more sanguine than heretofore. The daily explorations of sacred texts and other writings is of the essence in the quest for the spiritual being. Bitterness has receded-almost extinct. And for all that, thanks to the Almighty!

The Managing Director

I have been aware of spirituality in people since early childhood, that is, spiritual power, presence, essence, divine consciousness. My Roman Catholic upbringing did not help me understand and develop my spirituality. Instead the Church tried to trap my spirit, corrupt it with fear, guilt and ignorance and enslave it to its institutional control. There was no room for a free spirit.

I was much more attracted to the spiritual and religious beliefs and practices of Hindus, Buddhists, Aboriginies, Celtic monks, Hopi Indians and Atlanteans. Anything but Roman

Catholicism and the arrogance of empirical scientists, and anything that would show me more about what I knew to exist in me, in others and in the universe, i.e. a spiritual energy or power that was operating in other dimensions beyond the Third Dimension. I'm happy to describe it as Divine Consciousness or universal consciousness. I have always been comfortable in that knowledge and belief. So I was aware of spirituality but I did not know how to use it, or tap into it.

In business we meet all sorts of people, horrible and nasty, black-spirited people, along with the good ones, but we have to deal with them all on a daily basis. In the modern competitive global workplace it would be very unusual for spirituality to be cited in the corporate mission statement. It certainly wasn't cited in ours.

Despite being aware of spirituality I was unable to prevent a situation developing where our successful business partnership and friendship of seventeen years was about to implode leaving two people very angry towards each other. Gone was the understanding, compassion, patience, trust, respect and friendship that had built the business. We were both prepared to part and go in separate directions carrying a load of baggage. I was very angry and I had lost trust. My partner was the same. We were very stressed and acrimonious with each other. It continued like that for more than five years.

Many attempts were made to try to define the problems between us but this failed. There was something much more serious and, perhaps, sinister affecting us.

As a last ditch attempt, we asked an HR consultant, to get involved. I expected a clinical report saying that I was right, or mostly right, and that my business partner would be advised to make most of the changes. I thought that perhaps then we could try to get the business together again. In my mind, it was all very strategic and intellectual.

To my surprise we were both asked to first look at ourselves and then to look at each other in a spiritual sense before trying to deal with the problem elements of the business. It was not easy at the beginning, but it was definitely the right route to take. We were asked to trust another intelligence, not an intellectual one, but a spiritual one.

The counselling sessions were, for the most part, enjoyable. Tempers did flare where either or both of us was not willing to let go. Letting go and just trusting was difficult.

Over a period of six months, with dedicated application of the new rules of thinking and behaviour that we had been given, we learned to trust each other again, to respect each other's values, to cooperate and identify real needs across the board. Best of all we have learned to cooperate spiritually. We now hold a joint daily spiritual reading in the office to begin each day. Gone are the shouting matches and bouts of anger to be replaced by a peaceful cooperative work environment. I would like to have discovered how to tap into our spiritual intelligence long ago.

Today we are still business partners operating with a real peace of mind, or inner peace. We are much more relaxed as people and this reflects positively within the office and with our customer base. By being aware of spirituality and practising daily spiritual readings, meditation and breathing I can operate at a highly productive level with more trust and patience. I now bring compassion into my decision-making and contractual affairs. There is real pay off for me, with increased energy levels and creative output.

Due to the real peace of mind that I now experience, relationships and communications in the business operate much more smoothly. This gives me ammunition to deal with those horrible and nasty black-spirited people that I referred to earlier, but most importantly it prevents me from re-visiting that state of black-spiritedness and becoming one of them again.

The Teacher and Mother

As a child, I was fun, yet shy, lacking confidence and unable to speak up for myself. This continued into my adult life, my marriage and work. After many years of acquiescing to others and internalising my own frustrations and anger, the pressure became too much. I was giving into the views of my husband, my colleagues, my boss, even when I felt very differently to them. Worse still, I was venting some of the frustration I felt towards those I taught *and* my own children. I had to find a way to live truthfully *vis-à-vis* my own emotions without creating the unmerciful conflict I had experienced as a child watching my mother and father deal with their conflicts. I turned to God.

I prayed and experienced a tremendous peace and sense of a benevolent presence. I took to reading spiritual books and Scripture. I applied the lessons from the books and scriptures to my daily life: for example, when faced with a situation or person, I would feel my natural reactions bubbling up. But I would deliberately choose not to respond in this old pattern. Rather, I would respond using the approach I had read about. was astounded at home liberating this was. Each day became a drama as I interacted with Life, letting my natural reactions come to the surface (sometimes feeling the awful fear or anxiety of these reactions), then choosing to respond in a way the spiritual books or scriptures suggested. It was some clean up – and it is still going on! So, instead of getting upset with my colleagues, or those I taught, or even my husband and children, I would let go that reaction and choose a more appropriate one. Often, I would ask God to simply release in me His attitudes to a person or situation. I became a changed person using this simple technique. Where I had lacked assertiveness, over a short period of time, it seemed that this indwelling Presence released in me, at my request, His assertiveness (which I found to be so gracious, direct, honest yet giving dignity to the other). Where I had been shy, especially meeting strangers, now, using this process, I would experience a new-found strength and sociability. My rapport with those I taught escalated. My relationships with colleagues blossomed: they involved me more, no longer feeling that they had to 'dance gingerly' around me.

I have become such a relaxed person because now, when there is a work problem, I simply have a spiritual board meeting with God (whom I see as Love), hand it over to Him ('in the Name of Jesus' as I learned from the books) and then expect to see a successful result. It always comes, and it is always 'win-win' – for the other person(s) and for me. If I have a people problem, I do the same. I no longer shoulder the burden of the problem. I hand it over to God. Because I am more relaxed, people feel more relaxed in my company, those I teach achieve far better results (more 'A' grades regularly cropping up) and my fun side has come right out so that my colleagues, husband and children really enjoy me. I am such a fulfilled person since I connected with my Spiritual Source.

AFTERWORD

Beloved, I wish above all things
That you prosper and be in health
As your soul prospers
3 John 2

The issue of provision

Quantum theory has been bringing mankind's thinking out of the clutches of a model of the world that is four hundred years behind current science. However, so embedded is the general psyche of man in this outdated model[1] that the collective thinking of mankind is blocking the complete transition over to the quantum model[2], because in that model, scientists have found that thought affects the material world.

One thing is known and that is that each individual can help break the hold of the Newtonian model on the collective thinking of mankind by taking individual responsibility for the quality of his/her thoughts. This we can do by embarking on a long psychological trek, making the 180 degree turn from our thought life being affected by the material world on the one hand (Newtonian model), to our thoughts affecting the material world (quantum model) on the other. Along this trek we experience doubts, worries, anxieties, fears, catastrophic thinking, negativity, destructiveness and conditional love. Why? Because the Newtonian model is built on fear: Believing that the only things that exist are what we see, feel, hear, taste and touch, the Newtonian model tells us that what's in our planet is all we've got. So, armed with that mentality, we grab, hoard, 'save up for a rainy day' and protect what we have with alarms and insurances. What if this object is taken from me? Will I be able to get another? What if there are no others to get? What if I lose a limb?

The Newtonian model is like a psychological law of gravity: it pulls us down with its underpinning doubts and worries; it strangles and immobilises us with the negative movies it runs in our heads – those 'what ifs' – and it puts 'the final nail in our coffin' by a) having us see relationships in a conditional way (so we adopt a balance sheet approach to people) and b) telling us that our thoughts about people do not affect them. And so, we maltreat the very sources of succour and love that could sustain us in this model of life. By training us to be controlled by the evidence of our five senses, the Newtonian model strips us of control because we feel 'it's them out there' that is the problem, 'it's the weather', 'it's the economic downturn'. We become victims – and our cinema, theatre, television and newspapers foster that Newtonian view. The quantum model, on the other hand, sparks in us enormous hope, control and creativity. It tells us that our thoughts *do* affect things, situations and people – no matter where they are. This happens, it says, because we are all part of one big indivisible atomic whole – everything is made from the same atomic 'stuff' – and that atomic whole is intelligent and intelligently relates to us. This means that if we can access our thinking and clean out the limiting, negative mind sets (the ones we know are there and the ones we don't know are there) – like clearing a site in order to build a new house – then we can begin the exciting job of creating the kind of health, life, relationships and wealth we want. Just as when building a house we bring in an architect, so we must see ourselves as the architects of our own realities.

This is a very hard message for someone deep in the Newtonian model, because we have all seen tragedies – talented youngsters losing their limbs as a result of meningitis; young people dying of cancer. We all know of the 27 million women and children who are traded as slaves, and we too often witness wars throughout the world. These are hard facts – but they are facts in a model of the world that says we must use things external to ourselves to provide for ourselves. The quantum model says this is not so. Professor Francisco Varela, the distinguished professor of cognitive science and epistemology at the École Polytechnique and the Institute of Neuroscience in Paris, says '…what we are talking about is brand new territory – like exploring a new continent. Cognitive scientists are like sixteenth-century explorers looking at the early maps of America. The maps are probably wrong in many respects, but at least we know the continent exists. Once you appreciate that the nature of our world, our universe, is non-substantial, yet exists, then you immediately open up to the possibilities – possibilities to create and to change…. The fact is our language and our nervous system combine to constantly construct our environment…We lay the path down by an accumulation of recurrent human practices.'[3]

It is very clear that there is an urgent need for mankind to explore conclusively what quantum physics can teach about a different way of providing for ourselves: because provision is the big issue. One of the best companies for bringing spiritual intelligence into the workplace was so badly hit by the US economic slowdown that its shareholders have cleared out the old senior management team and brought in a new team whose ethos is bottom-line only management. Tens of thousands of jobs were lost throughout the Western world in a single week as a result of the attacks on the US. According to the Newtonian model this is a very bleak situation. But if we knew of a more sophisticated way of providing for ourselves…?

What can the quantum model tell us about how to provide for ourselves? Many authors have written about provision using the system of creation laid down by quantum physics: Catherine Ponder, Wayne Dyer and Deepak Chopra[4] have all written marvellously clear books on the issue of supply – although Catherine Ponder was writing in 1964, – well before any mainstream quantum thinking on the subject. Jesus himself said: 'Have faith in God. For assuredly I say to you, *whosoever* says to this mountain "Be removed and be cast into the sea," and does not doubt in his heart but believes that *those things he says will be done,* he will have whatsoever he says.'[5] So, we are back again at the issue of removing doubt. The Christian author and businessman Charles Capps[6] has written powerfully simple texts on the creative power of words and the spiritual laws of supply. His material would be corroborated by the findings of quantum physicists. Unless we urgently deal with how our new understanding of the design of this planet tells us to supply our needs, we will all be locked in the inevitable conflicts, power struggles and destruction which people, embedded in the Newtonian model, are convinced are the only way to create peace and provision on this earth.

The issue of time

Psychologists have long told us that it takes three weeks of exposure to an idea or factor for a minimum of one hour for that idea or factor to penetrate the subconscious mind, and that it is the subconscious mind that controls our behaviour.[7] We have created a society addicted to soap operas, television dramas, cinema, music and literature which are all coming from the Newtonian base. The Japanese Science Council has made it clear that we have only until 2050 before our planet can no longer sustain life. So, we have less than fifty years to change our thinking: we must work together on this – individual with individual, community with community, nation with nation – otherwise the spiritual intelligence we will be practising will not be on this earth, this three-dimensional plane, but in another life, another plane. Do *your* bit: change *your* thinking.